Palgrave Studies in Economic History

Palgrave Studies in Economic History is designed to illuminate and enrich our understanding of economies and economic phenomena of the past. The series covers a vast range of topics including financial history, labour history, development economics, commercialisation, urbanisation, industrialisation, modernisation, globalisation, and changes in world economic orders.

More information about this series at
http://www.palgrave.com/gp/series/14632

Ivan Luzardo-Luna

Colombia's Slow Economic Growth

From the Nineteenth to the Twenty-First Century

palgrave
macmillan

Ivan Luzardo-Luna
London School of Economics and Political Science
London, UK

ISSN 2662-6497 ISSN 2662-6500
Palgrave Studies in Economic History
ISBN 978-3-030-25754-5 ISBN 978-3-030-25755-2 (eBook)
https://doi.org/10.1007/978-3-030-25755-2

Cover illustration: Antiqua Print Gallery / Alamy Stock Photo

This Palgrave Pivot imprint is published by the registered company Springer Nature Switzerland AG.
The registered company address is: Gewerbestrasse 11, 6330 Cham, Switzerland

For my parents Martha and Pablo,
And for my wife Angelica

Preface

The idea of writing this book came after I taught an introductory course on economic history called 'The internationalization of economic growth, 1870 to the present day' at the London School of Economics. Several of the classes' discussions focused on the spread of general purpose technologies as drivers of economic growth. In that sense, those economies that saw an economic take-off in the late nineteenth century were those that were able to absorb steam, the general purpose technology of the industrial revolution. Likewise, the economic growth of the twentieth century was propelled by the diffusion of mass production technology, while since the 1990s, ICTs have become an essential driver of economic expansion.

In trying to establish the parallels of such processes in Colombia's history, it became evident to me that each one of these three technological waves came to that country very late. To understand the reasons behind such tardy behaviour, it is worth noting that other Latin American countries were able to take advantage of these technological waves. Argentina quickly absorbed steam technology in the 1880s and built a world-class railway network. Mexico started using mass production technology on a significant scale in the 1930s and became an important exporter of manufactured goods during the Second World War. Chile conducted an early economic liberalisation and implemented structural reforms in the 1980s, which allowed it to gain large investments in ICTs in the 1990s, propelling its service sector in the first two decades of the twenty-first century. These three successful examples of countries with the same colonial origin indicate that the reasons for slow economic growth go beyond institutional path dependency.

The economic slowdown Colombia has experienced since 2015 led to many observers putting forward productivity stagnation as the most critical reason behind Colombia's low potential growth. The productivity problem, however, has been a pattern of the Colombian economy since the late nineteenth century, and therefore, the study of economic history is useful to find a convenient solution. The slow productivity growth is ultimately the slow technological transfer or the delays to embracing the general purpose technologies.

The book is also the result of the exchange of ideas with many people. I would like to thank Antonio Celia for our long conversations about Colombia. Also, I would like to acknowledge and thank Juliana Jaramillo, who helped me to think about this book and generously shared a lot of historical statistics. In writing this book, the discussions at the office with my PhD colleagues Mauricio Canals, David Escamilla, and Enrique Jorge-Sotelo, who helped me to compare the Colombian case with others in Latin America, were essential. Likewise, I would also like to thank Edoardo Altamura, Sebastian Alvarez, Roy Miller, and Martin Monsalve, for their comments and conversations in workshop on the Latin American 1980s debt crisis at Oxford. Feedback from Andrew Primmer was also important due to his exceptional knowledge on the history of railways in Colombia.

I would also like to thank, for the conversations on this book, Eduardo Posada-Carbo, Enrique de la Rosa, Andrés López, Rafik Neme, and Sebastian Nieto, and many others that I am probably forgetting at this moment.

I would also like to thank Professor Kent Deng, the editor of Palgrave Studies in Economic History for his valuable feedback, as well as an anonymous referee. I would like to especially thank Laura Pacey and Ruth Noble, economics commissioning editors, who believed in this project. Likewise, I thank Clara Heathcock, Sophia Siegler, and Mark Freeman for their support in producing this book.

From the bottom of my heart, I would like to thank my parents Martha and Pablo for their permanent encouragement and sharing with me their anecdotes about the Colombian economy in the import substitution era. I could not have written this book without the unconditional support of my wife Angelica, whom I sincerely thank for her patience and love.

London, UK Ivan Luzardo-Luna

Contents

List of Figures

List of Tables

CHAPTER 1

The Particular Colombian Case in Latin America: A Singular Path with the Same Results

Abstract Despite similarities with other countries in the Latin America, Colombia's trajectory to development has been unique. If we need to oversimplify why the main Latin American countries do not yet have advanced economies, the short answer would be: deep and frequent economic depressions. If Colombia did not experience a depression since 1903, why did not this country do better?

Colombia's problem is that it historically grew driven by input factors (capital and labour) accumulation rather than by productivity, which has remained stagnant for long periods. Productivity growth has depended on countries' capacity to embrace technological progress. This book analyses how Colombia missed three technological waves of the last three centuries: steam, mass production, and Information and Communication Technology (ICT), and compares it with Argentina, Mexico, and Chile, respectively.

Keywords Economic growth • Productivity • General purpose technology • Steam • Mass production • ICTs

The economic history of Colombia is a story of a country that has swung between long periods of slow growth and short cycles of accelerated economic expansion. This unbalanced performance resulted in Colombia

I. Luzardo-Luna, *Colombia's Slow Economic Growth*,
Palgrave Studies in Economic History,
https://doi.org/10.1007/978-3-030-25755-2_1

being classified a middle-income country in 2016. Its income per capita is similar to other Latin American countries such as Brazil or Peru, but below Argentina, Chile, and Mexico.

Despite similarities with other countries in the region, Colombia's trajectory to development has been unique within Latin America. If we need to oversimplify why the main Latin American countries do not yet have advanced economies, the short answer would be: deep and frequent economic depressions, brought about to a large extent by macroeconomic mismanagement.

Depressions are characterised by profound economic decline, and are not very common throughout economic history, or at least since the dawn of the twentieth century onwards. Unlike recessions or normal business cycle fluctuations, a depression has long-lasting consequences in production capacity, employment, and, in some extreme cases, political stability. There is not a precise definition for a depression in quantitative terms, but some scholars use a decline in the real GDP per capita of more than 10% as rule of thumb.

Following this rule, Colombia has not experienced a depression since 1903, a rare exception in Latin America. The country has enjoyed relative macroeconomic stability in a region of the world where hyperinflation, debt crises, and sudden shrinking in the income per capita has been ever present. The Colombian case is a story of a country where economic booms have been very moderate, but economic progress has been constant since the early twentieth century.

Figure 1.1 contrasts the evolution of the GDP per capita between Colombia and the three largest economies in Latin America (except Brazil): Argentina, Chile, and Mexico, from 1905 up to 2016. These three countries had an income per capita significantly higher than Colombia in the early twentieth century, as the country was trapped in a long-lasting stagnation in the second half of the nineteenth century. Yet, Mexico had two major depressions at the dawn of the twentieth century—1910–1916 (the Mexican Revolution), and 1926–1936 (the Cristero War and the Great Depression)—which led to fall behind Colombia in 1927. Certainly, the Cristero War and the Great Depression were intense crises, as GDP per capita declined 31% between 1926 and 1932, in the middle of political instability generated by the civil war. Mexico was to have another major depression in the 1980s, as the real GDP per capita declined by 22% between 1981 and 1988, in the so-called *Latin America lost decade*.

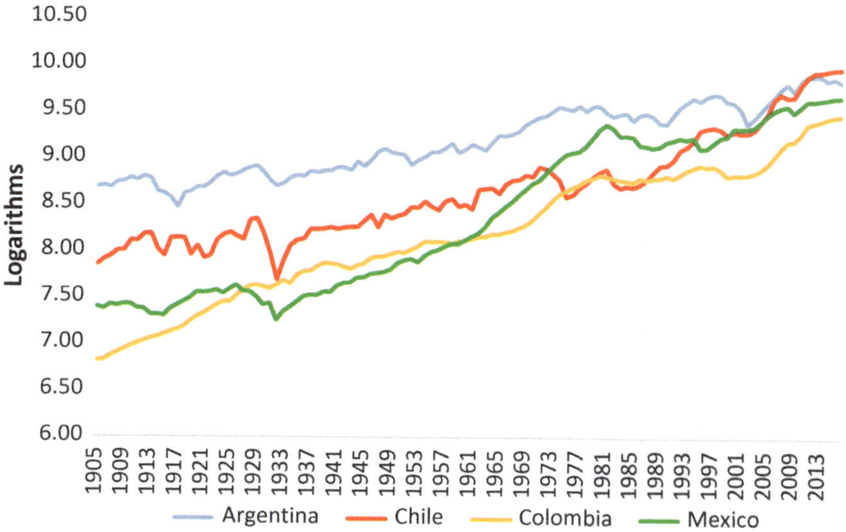

Fig. 1.1 Real GDP per capita at 2011 US$ prices (logs), 1905–2016 (Source: Maddison Project Database, Version 2018. Bolt, Jutta, Robert Inklaar, Herman de Jong, and Jan Luiten van Zanden (2018))

The southern cone countries performed well in the nineteenth century and, in particular, Argentina was a good candidate to converge with the United States or Britain as, in the early twentieth century, it had one of the highest GDPs per capita in the world. Yet, Argentina has experienced six major depressions since 1899, and this explains why it remained as a middle-income country in 2016. Likewise, Chile also experienced prosperity in the nineteenth century, thanks to an export-led growth model based on mining (particularly in nitrate). Chile, however, saw seven depressions since the dawn of the twentieth century.

The possibilities for becoming a fully developed country for Argentina, Chile, and Mexico were severely limited due to recurring depressions. Some of them were caused by external factors, such as sudden international price declines in commodities, but it was mostly by poor macroeconomic management. More prudent fiscal and monetary policies in these countries could have not completely prevented economic crises, but they would probably have been recessions instead of depressions. Table 1.1

Table 1.1 Major economic depressions, 1899–2016 (%)

Argentina			*Chile*			*Mexico*		
Number	*Year*	*Real GDP per capita decline*	*Number*	*Year*	*Real GDP per capita decline*	*Number*	*Year*	*Real GDP per capita decline*
1	1900	−15.3	1	1913–1915	−21.2	1	1909–1915	−11.9
2	1913–1917	−26.5	2	1919	−16.3	2	1926–1932	−31.4
3	1929–1932	−19.4	3	1921	−12.3	3	1981–1988	−22.4
4	1980–1982	−10.9	4	1929–1932	−48.0			
5	1987–1990	−10.5	5	1947	−12.4			
6	1998–2002	−26.8	6	1971–1975	−27.7			
			7	1981–1983	−18.2			

Sources: Estimated based on Maddison Project Database, Version 2018. Bolt, Jutta, Robert Inklaar, Herman de Jong, and Jan Luiten van Zanden (2018)

shows the main major depressions for Argentina, Chile, and Mexico from 1899 onwards.

The case in Colombia is quite different to the other major Latin American countries. For instance, the Great Depression of 1929 saw an income per capita reduction of 48%, and 19% for Chile and Argentina, respectively. On the other hand, Colombia had a very mild recession with the GDP per capita declining by just 3.8% between 1929 and 1931. Certainly, Colombia avoided depressions in the twentieth century, but its growth rates were so low; therefore, it was not enough to transform it into an advanced economy. That is very different from Argentina, Chile, and Mexico. Without their severe economic depressions, and everything else remaining constant, these countries probably would have become advanced economies or would be very close to achieving such status. This is not the case for Colombia, where other factors besides macroeconomic stability were obviously an issue.

1.1 Colombian Growth: Stable but Poor

Colombia's growth trend has certainly been stable. Yet, the outcome has been very similar to the regional average or, more accurately, worse than countries such as Argentina, Chile, or Mexico. This can be seen by analysing Fig. 1.2, which represents the GDP per capita in 2017 for the main economies in Latin America. Colombian income per capita that year was just 59% and 69% of the Chilean and Argentinian figures, respectively. This lag in development is especially interesting because, despite all of the turbulence and crises in the southern cone countries, they still appeared richer than Colombia.

Colombia's economic performance looks even worse if comparisons are made beyond Latin America. Figure 1.3 shows Colombia's GDP per capita relative to that of the United States, between 1905 and 2016. Here, it can be observed that, despite an acceleration of economic growth in Colombia in the early twentieth century, the convergence with North America ceased in the early 1930s. From the early 1930s onwards, the Colombian economy entered into a pattern of slow growth, which persisted over the remainder of the century, with the notable exception of the

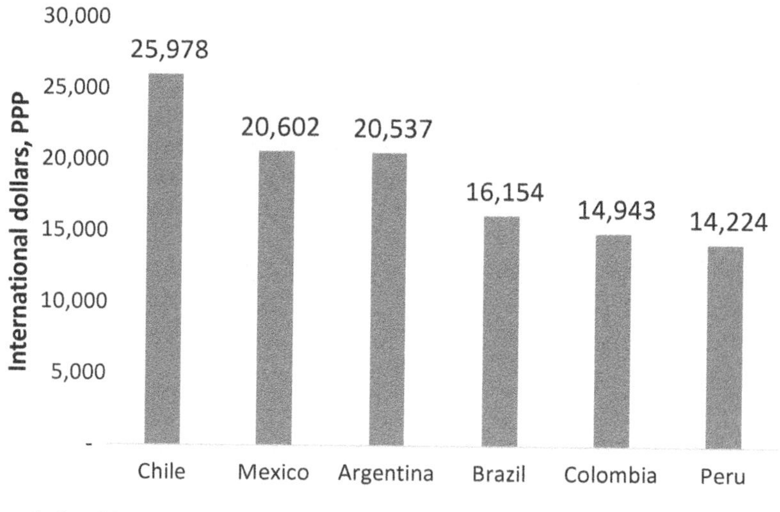

Fig. 1.2 GDP per capita 2018, current prices: purchasing power parity (International dollars per capita) (Source: International Monetary Fund. *World Economic Outlook* (April 2019))

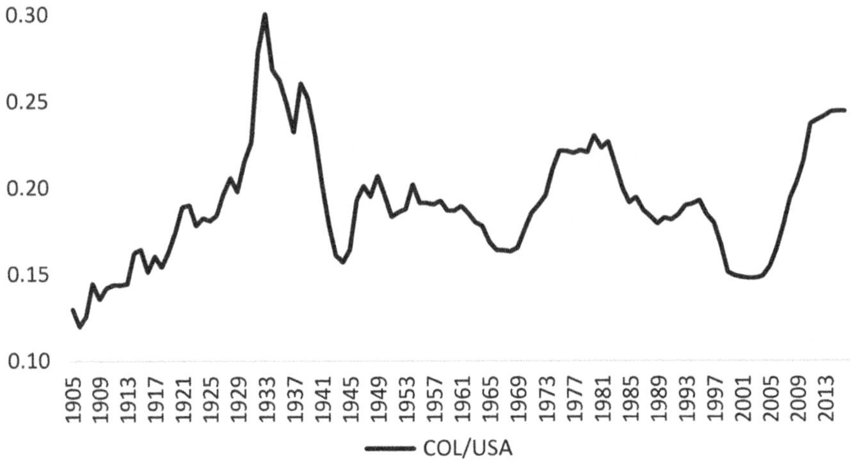

Fig. 1.3 Colombia's GDP per capita relative to that of the United States, 1905–2016 (Source: Maddison Project Database, Version 2018. Bolt, Jutta, Robert Inklaar, Herman de Jong, and Jan Luiten van Zanden (2018))

first half of the 1970s. Such poor economic performance made the chances of catching up with North America very remote. Indeed, the relationship between the GDP per capita of the two countries only changed with the dawn of the twenty-first century, when Colombia's economy started to pick up again, giving Fig. 1.3 the U-shaped profile between 1932 and 2011.

Colombia's economic performance was not just poor when compared to the United States as the technological leader of the last two centuries, but also to some countries, Colombia appeared to be poorer than it had been in the 1950s. Figure 1.4 shows Colombia's GDP per capita in relation to South Korea. Again, the results are disappointing. In 1951, Colombia's GDP per capita was almost threefold higher than that of South Korea but, in 2016, the percentage for Colombia compared to the GDP per capita of South Korea was just 36%.

1.2 Why Colombia Did Not Do Better? A Productivity Problem

If Colombia did not experience frequent and deep economic depressions, if the macroeconomic management was relatively prudent, and even when democracy (despite all the problems with security) survived from the

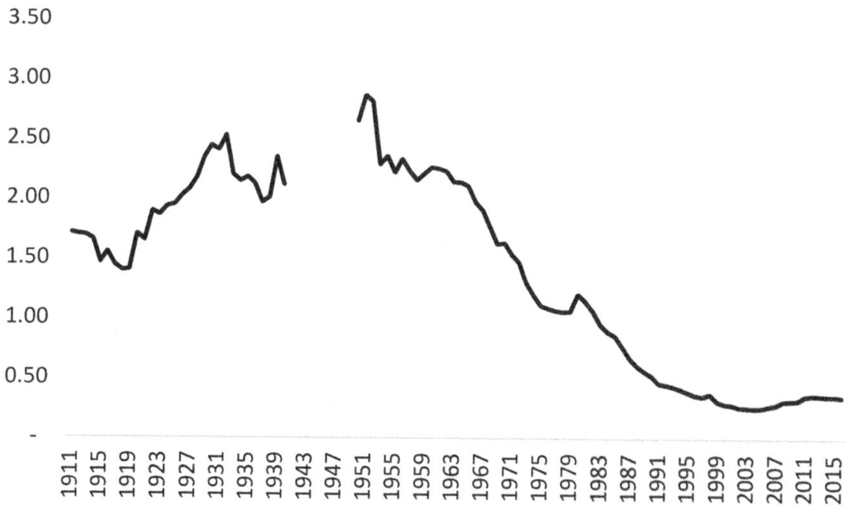

Fig. 1.4 Colombia's GDP per capita relative to that of South Korea, 1911–2016 (Source: Maddison Project Database, Version (2018). Bolt, Jutta, Robert Inklaar, Herman de Jong, and Jan Luiten van Zanden (2018))

nineteenth century, why didn't the country do better? This is the fundamental question in this book.

There are two ways how an economy can grow; either by increasing the input factors (capital and labour), or by using them in a more efficient way (increasing productivity). In that sense, there are three drivers of economic growth: investment (higher capital), employment (higher labour), and productivity (using the same capital and labour in a more efficient way). The latter, which is boosted with technology, has been the missing factor in Colombia's growth.

Since the seminal works elaborated on by Robert Slow, the economic growth models have highlighted technology as productivity's driver, and the final force of economic progress. With different perspectives and nuances, most such models conclude that the only way to sustain an increase in income per capita in the long run is through technological evolution and advancement. In fact, some influential observers maintain that recent moderate economic growth in the west is due to a lack of major technological breakthroughs, which boost revolutionary productivity like steam or electricity did in the last few centuries.

The question regarding why some countries do not take full advantage of the opportunities opened by technology is one of the most important aspects in economics as a discipline. A highly influential piece of literature states that the ultimate factors which underlie economic growth are institutions. Important as they are, institutions can change by historical circumstance, which is why the path dependency assumption, under what institutions remain stable over time, presents some constraints.

Against the long-held view, institutional path dependency cannot be thought of as a sole reason to fully explain Colombia's poor economic performance. This theory is suitable for explaining why rich countries remain richer than developing ones. In other words, why it was that North America, Western Europe, and Japan were able to make use of the opportunities presented by the industrial revolution, and became advanced economies, while the rest of the world struggled in achieving the same. Such theories, however, do not apply when trying to address why some countries, such as the Asian 'Tigers', were able to fully develop as advanced economies over such a short period of time. Factors such as institution or geography struggle to offer a convincing explanation for a country's full transition from low to high income.

A good experiment could control by institutions in order to know what other factors affect the economy. Comparing different regions within the same country, where most regions share the same institutions, could be a good approximation. As this is not possible for a country, the approach used in this book is to compare Colombia with countries with similar institutions, culture, and colonial origins. These countries are Argentina, Chile, and Mexico. Using them as benchmarks, it is possible to explore if there was a share of growth which does not depend on institutional path dependency, or in other words, if Colombia could have had higher growth rates besides its so-called *extractive institutions* (Acemoglu, Johnson, & Robinson, 2001). To be sure, this book is not dismissing the importance of institutions, but it explores the possibilities for growth besides them. Once progress has consolidated, institutions can evolve in the right direction.

Economic growth also has depended on countries' capacity to embrace technological breakthroughs. Technological progress is far from a linear path, and history shows that relevant changes occur in 'waves' (Lipsey, Carlaw, & Bekar, 2005). In this sense, a specific technological wave offers the possibility for accelerated economic growth in a determined period of time, which essentially ends with the arrival of the next technological wave.

This book follows a standard Solow-Swan model, where economic growth depends on inputs growth (capital and labour) and productivity. Analysing the four economies covered in this book, it can be concluded that Colombia essentially grew driven by inputs accumulation rather than productivity, which has remained stagnant for long periods. On the other hand, Argentina, Chile, and Mexico have had specific periods where both inputs and productivity expanded evenly, which allowed these countries to enjoy significant prosperity which transformed their economies. Yet, such fast-growth periods did not last long enough for these countries to shift into being fully developed.

1.3 Three Latin American Economic Miracles and a Chronically Tardy Country

As it has been noted in this chapter, Argentina, Chile, and Mexico had periods of fast economic growth, which can be classed as 'economic miracles'.

Argentina had an economic miracle between 1870 and 1910, a period commonly known as the *Belle-Époque*. Over those 40 years, Argentina achieved one of the highest income per capita statistics in the world. The Argentinean miracle is explained to a large extent by this country successfully integrating into the liberal order of the world by an export-led growth model. In achieving this goal, the country took full advantage of the general purpose technology which enabled economic growth at that time: steam. Argentina saw a massive expansion in railways, and the arrival of refrigerated shipping allowed a significant boom in the frozen and chilled meat industries.

Mexico's economic miracle started in the 1930s and lasted up to the 1970s. During this period, Mexico's wealth grew by increasing its industrial capacity following initially an inward-looking industrialisation in the 1930s, and a massive industrial export expansion during the Second World War. Here, the enabling technology was mass production, and it allowed Mexico to experience significant prosperity until 1980, when this country fell into an economic depression known as the 'Latin America debt crisis'.

Chile's economic miracle started in 1985 and lasted until 2013. Throughout this period, the real GDP per capita almost trebled, fuelled by successful economic liberalisation and incorporation into the world economy in the 1980s. This country took full advantage of the possibilities opened by the new wave of globalisation, enabled to a large extent by the development of Information and Communication Technology (ICT), which has been an enabling general purpose technology since the 1990s onwards. Despite Chile's economic growth, relying to a large extent on commodities, this country was successful in modernising important services such as retail and banking by a strong building of ICT capital since the second half of the 1990s.

On the other hand, Colombia arrived late in each one of these technological waves: steam, mass production, and ICT. The following chapters examine how the country came late in each one of these technological revolutions, thereby missing the opportunity for increased economic growth. Also, the Colombian case is contrasted against each one of these Latin American economic miracles in order to understand the economic reasons behind these processes and how Colombia lacked the economic pre-conditions for such technological leaps.

References

Acemoglu, D., Johnson, S., & Robinson, J. (2001). The Colonial Origins of Comparative Development: An Empirical Investigation. *The American Economic Review, 91*(5), 1369–1401.

International Monetary Fund. (2019, April). *World Economic Outlook.*

Lipsey, R., Carlaw, K., & Bekar, C. (2005). *Economic Transformations: General Purpose Technologies and Long Term Economic Growth.* Oxford: Oxford University Press.

Maddison Project Database, Version 2018. Bolt, Jutta, Robert Inklaar, Herman de Jong and Jan Luiten van Zanden. (2018). *Rebasing 'Maddison': New Income Comparisons and the Shape of Long-Run Economic Development.* Retrieved from https://www.rug.nl/ggdc/historicaldevelopment/maddison/releases/maddison-project-database-2018

CHAPTER 2

The Price of the *Regeneration*: How Colombia Missed the Belle-Époque, 1870–1914

Abstract The *Belle-Époque* (1870–1914) was a period of great prosperity for those economies which incorporated steam technology into their national economies. The main way in which steam enhanced progress at that time was through the railways, which allowed the consolidation of an export-led economic growth model.

In this period, Colombia missed a golden opportunity for its economic take-off. Unlike Argentina, Colombia's real GDP per capita remained stagnant throughout the late nineteenth century. The former country was able to build an extensive railway network, while the latter increased its kilometres of railways very slowly, which determined its poor export growth. Colombia's incapability to build railways was due to the fact that it could not attract foreign investors, as the government's lack of commitment in honouring the external debt.

Keywords Export-led growth • Steam • Railways • External debt • Argentina

The Belle-Époque (1870–1914) was a period of massive economic expansion for those economies integrated into the world economy. It was during this period, when the possibilities for economic prosperity opened by the industrial revolution spread beyond Britain via several channels, such

I. Luzardo-Luna, *Colombia's Slow Economic Growth*,
Palgrave Studies in Economic History,
https://doi.org/10.1007/978-3-030-25755-2_2

as trade, capital flows, and international migration. The enabling general purpose technology which allowed such a transformation was steam, particularly its use in transportation.

Latin America also benefited from the possibilities created by this first wave of globalisation, and some countries enjoyed sustained progress following an export-led growth model based on commodities. Such a model consists of boosting economic growth by exports, achieving volumes, specialisation, and economies of scale, large enough to induce an economic take-off. This export-led growth model cannot be oversimplified to one where the emerging economies in the New World were just commodities exporters with less than significant technological progress. The actual fact is that for those countries in Latin America which successfully integrated into the world economy saw significant productivity gains by the incorporation of steam technology into their national economies.

The main way in which steam enhanced progress in Latin America at that time was through the railways, and this had a profound spill-over effect which positively transformed the region's potential for economic growth. This transport breakthrough forged a mobility and trade revolution, which not only linked Latin American exports with customers in Europe and North America, but also allowed the emergence of real national economies for the first time. The economic history of Latin America hitherto was one of economically fragmented countries with several local markets poorly integrated among them. The railway was a watershed that enabled many Latin American economies to progress rapidly.

Railways resulted in a new mobility revolution, and allowed Latin American primary goods to reach European markets, bringing to the region not just payments in hard currencies, but also the much needed capital and skills to expand its production capacity. The abundance of land and natural resources to be exploited in the New World were attractive in the eyes of European traders and immigrants, as well as British investors. The availability of resources in the London capital market, plus the region's natural endowments, opened up the possibility for authentic economic miracles in the still-new Latin American republics. However, out of all of them, it was to be Argentina that was the only country to realise this potential.

Not all countries in the region benefited to the same degree from steam and the possibilities offered by the Belle-Époque. The actual fact was that Colombia missed a golden opportunity for structural economic transformation, and the economic take-off had to wait until the early twentieth century. Unlike the cases of several Latin American countries, Colombia's GDP remained stagnant (in per capita terms) throughout the late nineteenth century, and only grew sustained in the early twentieth century. The immediate reasons behind this stagnation were, among others, Colombia's poor physical and financial integration into the world economy. The ulterior cause was probably the triumph of the conservative ideas implemented during the period known as *La Regeneración* (The Regeneration), which ruled Colombia between 1878 and 1904, and delayed the integration of the country into the world economy.

2.1 Colombia's Economic Performance Throughout the Belle-Époque

Railways were a key prerequisite for the economic take-off during the export-led growth era, as they were the main way in which steam could be incorporated into national production, and this is what propelled exports. With most of the population and agricultural production existing in inland areas, overcoming geographical insolation was essential for economic development. In fact, it was only in the early twentieth century, when the government made significant investments in transportation, that Colombia experienced a sustained increase in its income per capita.

Table 2.1 shows the GDP per capita for Argentina, Chile, Colombia, and Mexico for the second half of the nineteenth century. While Colombia remained stuck in secular stagnation, the other three countries underwent substantial economic progress post 1870. It is worth noting that between 1850 and 1870, Colombia experienced significant economic growth with an increase per capita of 37.4%, almost the same as Chile, the regional leader for economic growth in that period. Such remarkable prosperity

Table 2.1 Real GDP per capita (USD $ 2011), 1850–1910

Country	*1850*	*1870*	*1890*	*1900*	*1910*
Argentina	2144	2514	4139	4925	6547
Chile	1011	1397	2174	2533	3355
Colombia	681	937	995	946	1080
Mexico	795	789	1184	1374	1690

Sources: Maddison Project Database, Version 2018. Bolt, Jutta, Robert Inklaar, Herman de Jong and Jan Luiten van Zanden (2018)

was generated by the large expansion of tobacco exports and, to a lesser extent, quinoa (Melo, 2015). Considering this fact, the initial conditions for economic growth after 1870 were not particularly adverse. The country already had an entrepreneurial group with some experience in trading with the rest of the world, and the federal-liberal ruling regime was aware that the path for prosperity was that of international trade. The laissez-faire doctrine was at the core of the liberal rule that governed Colombia between 1863 and 1878, an ideology that could have facilitated the country's integration into London's capital market. However, such a regime could not have been consolidated in the 1870s, when precisely steam technology opened the way for sustained economic growth.

Colombia's poor physical and financial integration into the world economy was certainly a central element in its secular stagnation between 1870 and 1910. The gap in kilometres of railways showed a significant difference between Colombia and the three other Latin American countries presented, as can be observed in Table 2.2. Contrasting Table 2.1 with Table 2.2, the link is evident between railway construction and economic growth in the late nineteenth century, as has been noted in abundant literature (Herranz-Loncan, 2011; Lewis, 1983; Summerhill, 2000, 2003).

Colombia increased its kilometres of railways very slowly, and this is what made it different from the other three countries. Despite being a country that accelerated its construction in the early twentieth century, the railway network was still not expansive enough to overcome its geographical insolation in 1910. Although some observers point out the absence of a commodity to export in a large enough scale as a constraint to Colombia's economic stagnation in the nineteenth century, it is also plausible to assume that this could not have been economically viable due to the high transportation costs at that time. A completely different story was the case for Argentina, which was able to build a truly extensive rail-

Table 2.2 Kilometres of railways, 1855–1910

Country	*1855*	*1870*	*1889*	*1900*	*1910*
Argentina	–	985	8255	16,767	27,713
Chile	81	727	3100	4354	5944
Colombia	78	103	371	568	988
Mexico	–	347	8600	13,585	19,748

Source: For 1855–1889: Poor (1889). For 1900–1910: MOxLAD (n.d.)

way network, and saw a massive increase in exports. These increases were initially in wheat, but this commodity was quickly overtaken by chilled meat, once refrigeration was possible with the development of electricity (Lewis, 2002).

Argentinian railways, funded mainly by British capital, were an essential component of this country's strong economic growth. More moderate, but still very significant, was the case of Mexico, a country whose GDP per capita was lower than that of Colombia in 1870. Mexico increased its railway network after the consolidation of the political regime known as *el Porfiriato* (1876–1911), which, like Argentina, managed to fund its railway expansion with foreign investment. In the case of Mexico, however, the origin of capital was more diversified with the United States and France also very much involved in the railway's construction.

The question as to why Colombia showed such poor economic performance between 1870 and 1910 leads necessarily to the question regarding why it was not able to build a railway network that was reasonable and workable. This latter question in turn leads us to ponder why the country could not attract the required, and very probable British, capital needed for its railway construction. If the causes for Colombia's late nineteenth century stagnation were inside the country, these were deeply linked with the London Stock Exchange, the main capital market in the world at that time. The two issues—railways and access to capital markets—were at the core of why Colombia did not seize the opportunity and the potential for economic growth offered by steam.

2.2 Colombia's Railways Between 1870 and 1914

One of the main flaws in the Colombian railway system during the export-led growth age was its fragmentation. Rather than being a proper network, railways were a patchy system of several disconnected lines that were complementary to steam navigation on the Magdalena, the main River of Colombia. Such a water route was the backbone of transport in Colombia from pre-colonial times as it connected the inland areas with the coast. Despite steam navigation being operated regularly since the 1850s (Melo, 2015), the depth of the Magdalena is very heterogeneous, and this is what constrained its navigability. The numerous sandbars and floods made steam navigation an inferior substitute for the railways, and made transport costly (Fig. 2.1).

Fig. 2.1 Colombian main cities and ports (Source: Elaborated based on layers at ArcGIS)

The Panama railway, which linked the two oceans, was the first in Colombia. The route, completed in 1856, was of major interest for the United States, as it was a convenient and affordable passage from the east coast to the recently incorporated California and other territories in the west. This railway, consisting of 78 kilometres, opened up many possibilities for Colombia, due to its huge potential for profit and strategic location. The actual fact is that it was these opportunities that were only marginally exploited by Colombia, who did not extend such line into the inland territories.

The second railway in Colombia was the Bolivar railway, also known as the Barranquilla railway, which linked Sabanilla on the Caribbean Sea with Barranquilla at the northern end of the Magdalena River. As well as the Panama, the Bolivar railway was profitable during its early years of operation, although certainly with a much lower traffic volume and revenue. The effect of the Bolivar railway on Colombia's economy was outstanding, and the main indicator of the magnitude of such transformation was Barranquilla's increase in population.

According to McGreevy (1971), who based his estimation on census data, in 1871–1872, Barranquilla's population was 11,595 inhabitants which was equal to 39% of Medellin, Colombia's second largest city and was the economic powerhouse from the second half of the nineteenth century up to the late twentieth century. McGreevy (1971) also estimated that in 1905, Barranquilla had 40,115 inhabitants, which was equal to 73% of Medellin's population. The transformation was certainly notable, and no other large city in Colombia experienced such exceptional growth throughout that period.

The success of the Barranquilla railway was due to its route linked the Magdalena River, and therefore the interior of the country, with a seaport. A framework where inland products can reach ports on the coast is the very essence of a railways' benefit success for a developing country in the context of export-led growth. The Barranquilla railway fixed an important problem which steam navigation on the Magdalena River could not solve, and that was quick access to the Atlantic Ocean, and this was fundamental for Colombia's integration with the world economy.

Panama and Barranquilla railways were followed by the Cucuta railway, which started construction in 1878 and was opened in 1888. This new route, of 55 kilometres, linked the north of Santander (East of Colombia) with the Zulia River on the border with Venezuela, which allowed access to the Atlantic Ocean throughout the Maracaibo Lake. As its two predecessors had done, the Cucuta railway linked the inland areas with a maritime port.

The three pioneering railways had in common that they were all short hauls and very close to the maritime ports, which is what explains their early profitability. The lines of the future would not have the same luck, as all them, except the short lines of La Dorada and Santa Marta, showed poor progress and could only be completed in the twentieth century. Table 2.3 summarises the railways initiated between 1850 and 1890. Despite the initial success of Panama, Barranquilla, and Cucuta, Colombia's long-distance lines showed a chronic pattern of slow progress and unfinished work.

The Cauca railway, also known as the Pacific railway, was projected to link Cali (on the Cauca River) with Buenaventura (on the Pacific Ocean) with a route extension estimated at 137.9 kilometres (Cisneros, 1878). The work was initiated in 1878 with the Cuban Engineer, Francisco Javier Cisneros as general director of the enterprise. Cisneros was also in charge of the construction of the Barranquilla railway and was involved in other railway projects in the country, for which he was already well positioned among the Colombian elite. Despite the initial optimism and support of

Table 2.3 Railways initiated from 1850–1890

Railway name	*Route*	*Year when works commenced*	*Initial projected extension (km)*	*Completed in 1890 (km)*	*Status at 1890*	*Rate of completion (%)*
Panama	Colón-Panamá	1850	78	78	Completed	100
Barranquilla	Barranquilla-	1869	27	27	Completed	100
Cucuta	Cucuta-Zulia River	1878	55	55	Completed	100
Antioquia	Medellin-Puerto Berrio	1874	201	48	Uncompleted	23
Pacific	Buenaventura-Cali	1878	137.9	52	Uncompleted	38
Santa Marta	Santa Marta-Cienaga	1882	33[a]	33	Completed	100
La Dorada	La Dorada-Honda	1882	15	15	Completed	100
Girardot	Girardot-Facacativa	1885	111	31	Uncompleted	28

Source: Elaborated based on Melo (2015) and Meisel, Ramirez, and Jaramillio (2014)
[a]This value is based on the original route established in the Law 53 of 1881

the Colombian government, after 14 years, this route had only progressed 27 kilometres.

In July 1882, the Cauca railway inaugurated a partial haul between Buenaventura, on the Pacific coast, and Cordoba (Correa, 2012). This route replaced navigation on the River Dagua, which could have led to some social savings. In its first year of operation, however, the Cauca railway suffered losses that were 75% higher than its revenue,[1] a fact that certainly did not favour the project's progression. In the face of their own financial problems and difficulties in gaining access to foreign capital, Cisneros sought for the contract to be terminated by the government. After Cisneros' petitioning at least three times, the government finally accepted his request in June 1885 (Correa, 2012). The whole route of the Cauca railway was only completed in the 1920s, when the Colombian government finally had enough financial resources via its own revenue and access to capital markets. Between 1872 and 1919, there had been seven concessioners, and all of them had not managed to complete the work (Pachon & Ramirez, 2006).

Similarly, The Antioquia railway was projected to link Medellin and Puerto Berrio on the Magdalena River with an extension of 201 kilometres.[2] The work was initiated in 1874 but after many years it made poor progress. In December 1883, the length that had been completed and put into operation accounted for just 32.5 kilometres.[3] This partial route generated significant losses, which again worked against not just the project's profitability but also reduced its credibility for investors. Between January and June 1883, the Antioquia railway generated losses that were 1577% higher than its modest revenue.

The unfinished works undoubtedly affected the Cauca and Antioquia railways. Colombia was able to build short-haul routes, but not long-haul railways, resulting in the persistence of physical fragmentation. Railways, rather than being a network, were isolated lines, which in some cases could not even reach the Magdalena River.

Instead of looking for the ports on the coast, the main purpose of the lines in the inland areas was to reach the Magdalena River. Once there, passengers and freight could continue on their way by steamer ship. Such a fragmented structure entailed significant cost, and it avoided taking

[1] Poor's Manual of Railways.

[2] Poor's Manual of Railways.

[3] Poor's Manual of Railways.

advantage of the so-called *network externalities*, which is at the very heart of a railway's benefits. *Network externalities* are the additional benefits received by current lines for the building of a new line. This latter factor increases the total network coverage, which makes the former more accessible, thereby increasing the amount of users. A pre-condition for such benefits, however, is the integration between railways lines.

In the late nineteenth century, Colombia's railways were far from enjoying *network externalities*, as the lines were largely left disconnected. Likewise, the main Colombian cities, such as Bogota, Medellin, Cali, and Bucaramanga, remained with poor access to the country's ports. The early railways improved the transport's conditions, but were far from overcoming the geographical barriers. In 1900, Colombia was almost a landlocked country, where the interior commodities were at a remote distance from the coast. This fact is what had led notable observers (Safford & Palacios, 2002) to put forward the notion that geographical dispersion was the main reason behind Colombia's slow economic development.

The poor ability of the inland regions to access to maritime ports was even noted by some international observers in the twentieth century, when Colombia's economic take-off had already started. *The Trade Information Bulletin No. 223*, was a publication of the Bureau of Foreign and Domestic Commerce for the Department of Commerce of the United States in 1924, based on the reports of the acting commercial attaché Carlton Jackson, the consuls in Bogota and Barranquilla, and the Vice Consul in Cartagena, page 16 of this document read as follows:

> *The 16 lines comprising the railway system of Colombia are all, with the exception of the Pacific Railroad, short disconnected lines with no direct rail connections with the seaports. Unfortunately, almost the whole scheme of railroad construction in Colombia has pertinaciously followed the idea of the Magdalena River as the main artery of transportation and ultimate destination rather than the seaports with unhappy results, as the navigation of the river is difficult and uncertain…*
>
> *The construction and location of lines has frequently been unduly influenced by local demands and not enough consideration has been given to the desirability of having through connections and avoiding transfer cargo. The lines connecting Bogota with the coast are very good examples of this lack of foresight. The line from Bogota to Facatativa is meter gauge; from there to Girardot on the Magdalena River it is 3-foot gauge, necessitating the transfer of all freight at Facatativa. Girardot is a point on the upper Magdalena, and a line could have been built from Facatativa at practically the same cost to some point on the*

> *lower river, thus avoiding the transfer of freight at Girardot to steamers for shipment to Beltran, where another transfer to rail is necessary to carry freight to La Dorada, the head of navigation on the lower river. At La Dorada freight is loaded onto steamers for shipment to Calamar or Barranquilla where it is again transferred to trains for Cartagena or Puerto Colombia on the coast.* (*Trade Information Bulletin, No. 223.* United States Department of Commerce, Latin America Division)

This analysis summarises two fundamental flaws in Colombia's railway system in the early twentieth century, which were even worse in the late nineteenth century: the lack of integration between the lines, and the poor access to maritime ports. Colombia has maintained for too long the Magdalena River as the backbone of its transportation system and delayed deep integration between its regions and the world economy, which had a negative impact on its prosperity. A route with high potential for overcoming the geographical divide between coast and the inland, without the involvement of costly and slow steam navigation on the Magdalena River, could have been a railway between Medellin and Cartagena. A plan to build such a route was part of the government projects list in the early twentieth century,[4] but unfortunately this line was never realised.

Why did the Colombian elite not build a main line which integrated the regional lines, thereby integrating the whole country? The actual fact is that the liberal regime of the early 1870s had a firm resolution to accomplish, at least partially, this goal. The liberals' plan, and probably their favourite infrastructure project, was the Northern railway, a route aimed at linking Bogota with the Magdalena River in Carare. The Northern railway was not a direct route to the coast, but the proposed track should pass through Boyaca and Santander before reaching the Magdalena River. Despite the flaw of not reaching the coast, this route could have integrated a significant part of Colombia's regions in the east of the country, and served as a base for further expansions.

The Minister of Finance in 1874, Aquileo Parra, who would be president of Colombia between 1876 and 1878, openly defended the project against critics such as the congressman Salvador Camacho Roldan's, who pointed out the government's difficulties in paying back the loan for funding the railway's construction (Junguito, 2018). It was also noted

[4] Bureau of Foreign and Domestic Commerce (1924). *The Trade Information Bulletin No. 223.* Department of Commerce of the United States.

that the project favoured only certain regions but was funded for the whole country, and this was opposed by other regions outside the route.

Due to the fiscal constraints and political instability which started from 1876, the Northern railway only started work in 1893, but only a short track up to Zipaquira was completed in 1898. The completed kilometres were only 47, which was approximately only 12% of the originally estimated 404 kilometres.[5] In the early twentieth century, the Northern railway existed as another isolated line, and as was the case for the Antioquia or Cauca railways, could not enjoy the benefits of '*Network Externalities*'.

The central question for Colombian railways seems to be, why only short distances on early tracks could be completed, while the long-distance lines remained unfinished? The answer very probably lies in financial constraints. Certainly, the economy did not have the capacity to command large investment projects, which demands enormous funds.

Due to its precarious economic development in the late nineteenth century, Colombia was far from having an internal capital market with enough resources to fund its railway construction plans. Such projects demanded the mobilisation of vast amounts of resources which could only be covered by foreign investors; without them, any plans for railway construction were unrealistic. Foreign capital was an inexorable partner for economic growth in the Belle-Époque, and the unfortunate relationship with it determined to a great extent, Colombia's incapability of creating any transport infrastructure which allowed a successful economic take-off as that which occurred in Argentina, Chile, and Mexico. Colombia could not attract foreign investors as its political elite did not understand the fundamental law in finance: the *risk-return trade off* principle. The second wave of railways, the long-distance lines, was probably not profitable enough to compensate for the high risk of investing in Colombia.

2.3 Colombia's Access to International Capital Markets

An essential mechanism for how the industrial revolution spread from Britain to the rest of the world was the flow of capital. British overseas investment was not only an important component of the economic upturn

[5] The number comes from the reports of Colombian Railways Company. Compañia Nacional del Ferrocarril del Norte (1875). *Informes sobre el Ferrocarril del Norte*. Ministerio de Hacienda y Crédito Público.

in countries such as the United States or Canada, but it was also vital for Latin America. Countries such as Argentina, Brazil, and Chile funded their railways mainly from British capital, while Colombia was unable to gain access to such funding. London was by far the primary capital market in the world in the late nineteenth century, which is why it is plausible to assume that any serious attempt to obtain foreign investment needed the approval of its stock exchange.

One of the fundamental laws in finance is the so-called the ***risk-return trade off*** principle, which maintains that an investment's return is negatively correlated with its risk. According to such a rule, the higher the risk, the higher the return. In other words, investors must be rewarded for taking a higher risk with a greater return, otherwise they will not have any incentive to lend as they could obtain the same profit from a safer asset.

According to the ***risk-return trade off*** principle, not all assets have the same return, as they all have different risks. Such a principle could also be extended to countries in the case of foreign investment or sovereign debt. In this case, a risky country naturally faces greater borrowing costs as they must compensate potential investors for the increased chance of their loans not being repaid.

Naturally, the high cost of borrowing is a common constraint for developing countries in obtaining credit. Only the most profitable projects have any real chance of obtaining credit. It is under such a framework, why it is understandable that the Panama railway did not suffer any inconvenience in obtaining investment that was needed for its construction, while the Pacific railway did not enjoy the same good fortune. Assuming that both projects face a similar risk, and they are in the same country, only the most potentially profitable one can attract interest from investors.

In solving the question as to why Colombia could not attract foreign capital investment, leads to necessarily analysing its borrowing costs, which certainly acts as a signal for its debtor behaviour and credibility. Figure 2.2 shows the sovereign bond yields for Argentina, Chile, Colombia, and Mexico between the years 1824 and 1914, which can be interpreted as a proxy of the countries' borrowing cost. As the theory predicts, not all countries faced the same borrowing costs, and certainly Colombia should have had to pay a higher price to obtain capital, and this explains why only a few railways that were short in length and neighbouring the coast, such as Panama's or Barranquilla's, could overcome such a barrier.

A bond yield is the proportion of its return against its market price. As both variables are essentially determined by the borrowers' credibility and

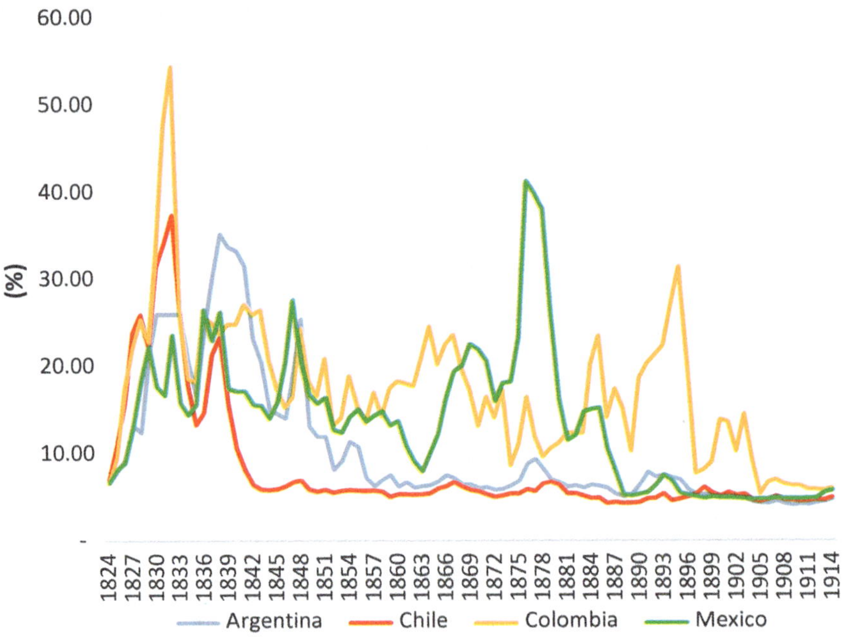

Fig. 2.2 Sovereign bond yields, 1824–1914 (Source: Global Financial Data Finaeon, n.d.)

Notes:

For Argentina: The Buenos Aires 6% Bonds of 1824 are used from 1824 to 1879; The Buenos Aires 6% Bonds of 1870 are used from 1880 to 1886; The Argentina 5% Bonds of 1886–1887 is used from 1887 to 1903; The Argentina 4% Railway Guaranteed Rescission Bond of 1896–1899 from 1904 to 1914; All bonds traded in London

For Chile: The Chile 6% Bond of 1822 is used from 1822 to 1859; The Chile 4.5% Bond of 1858 is used from 1859 to 1885; The Chile 4.50% Bond of 1885 (Redeemable 1935) is used from 1886 to 1888; The Chile 4.50% Loan of 1886 (Redeemable 1937) is used from 1888 to 1914; All bonds traded in London

For Colombia: The Colombia 6% Bonds of 1822 are used from 1822 to 1824; The Colombia 6% Bonds of 1824 is used from 1825 to 1842; The Colombia 6% Bonds of 1824 excluding Venezuela is used from 1842 to 1845; The Colombia New Granada 0.5% Active Debt Rising to 3% is used from 1845 to 1873; The Colombia 4.75% (prior 4.5%) New Granada Debt Converted Bond of 1873 is used from 1874 to 1897; The Colombia 1.5%–3% Consolidated External Debt Loan of 1896 is used from 1897 to 1914; All bonds traded in London

For Mexico: The Mexico 5% Bonds of 1824 are used from 1824 to 1825; The Mexico 6% Bonds of 1825 are used from 1826 to 1839; The Mexico 5% Consolidated Bonds of 1837 are used from 1839 to 1847; The Mexico 5% Bonds of 1846 are used from 1848 to 1852; The Mexico 3% Bonds of 1851 are used from 1852 to 1888; The Mexico 6% Consolidated Bonds of 1899 are used from 1888 to 1914; All bonds traded in London

its behaviour as debtor, the yield fluctuation leads us to examine foreign debt in the studied countries.

The story of foreign debt in Latin America commenced at the very beginning of the republics, as the first sets of credit were contracted for funding the independence wars (1810–1826). After the Napoleonic wars, Britain was consolidated as a global lender, opening London's financial markets for overseas governments and companies. British investors probably overestimated the 'new world's' wealth, as a significant amount of British foreign investment went to Latin America in the 1820s. Soon after such a substantial capital inflow to the region, the newly established Latin American countries were found to suffer from serious financial difficulties in servicing their external debt, and this was reinforced by the prolonged period of the independence wars. The panic of London in 1825 triggered a sudden suspension of capital inflow towards Latin America, and this impacted the already weak national treasures (Marichal, 2014). With still poor tax revenues in the newly independent countries, all Latin American countries, except Brazil, suffered from suspension of all payments until mid-1827 (Marichal, 2014).

The first Latin American country to reach an agreement with foreign lenders was Chile in 1842 (Marichal, 2014), which recognised the unpaid interest from 1826. As Fig. 2.2 shows, the four countries had a similar starting point, and their bond yields significantly increased after the 1827 suspension of payments. From 1842 onwards, however, Chile had a substantially lower rate, which could be interpreted as the market rewarding it for its exemplary behaviour. The 1842 agreement between Chile and its foreign lenders meant that this country could have much more affordable borrowing costs than the other three countries analysed. In 1844, the Chilean bond yields were below 6%, a favourable circumstance for the guaranteed return of 7%, which was the standard for foreign investment in railways in Latin America (Lewis, 1983; Pachon & Ramirez, 2006), and would have been attractive. Yet, the railway investment boom was still to come several years ahead as such technology only became widespread in the 1870s.

The Chilean example was followed by other countries in the region, such as Peru, which resumed its debt payments in 1849 (Marichal, 2014). Analysing Fig. 2.2, it can be observed that between 1850 and 1870, the Argentine bond yield declined and practically converged with the Chilean rate. This was as a result of an agreement between Argentina and its bondholders in 1857, under which this country resumed its debt payments.

It is worth noting that only after such an agreement could Argentina have a bond yield rate of lower than 7%, which appeared to be the critical threshold for railway construction. In the onset of the railways boom, Argentina was in a good position with the London capital market, which significantly reduced its borrowing costs, making a guaranteed investment return of 7% in railways an attractive option for British investors. The alignment between the arrival of a powerful general purpose technology, and the Argentinian pre-conditions to embrace this technology (access to foreign credit) created the conditions for what was probably the most impressive economic miracle in Latin American history.

Figure 2.2 also shows that the Colombian yield declined substantially from 23.8% in 1867, to 13.3% in 1870. Such movement probably signalled that the market was positively registering the efforts of the federal-liberal regime of reaching an agreement with the bondholders. Colombian bond yield in 1870 was at its lowest since 1826, but was still higher than that of Argentina and Chile, and what was probably more important was that it exceeded the 7% level. During the onset of the railway age, Colombia's borrowing costs were still very high.

Pachon and Ramirez (2006) maintain that the government offered favourable conditions to the railway concessioners such as land and a guaranteed return of 7%. According to them, the reason behind the poor quality of railway building in the late nineteenth and the early twentieth centuries, was a lack of clarity in the construction rules, which allowed the systematic breach of contracts by the concessioners and builders. As important as the clarity and the contracts were, Colombia's government was not offering terms that were attractive enough for serious entrepreneurs, but probably only for speculators and rent seekers.

A guarantee of 7% could have been seen as profitable from the Colombian policy-makers' eyes in the 1870s. That level, however, became significantly lower once the country's risk was taken into account at that time. The Colombian policy-makers of the late nineteenth century probably did not understand the *risk-return trade off* principle. A guarantee of 7% was attractive for countries such as Argentina or Chile because their borrowing costs were certainly lower. Colombia probably had at that time two ways of attracting foreign capital; either by reducing its borrowing costs, or by paying a higher return. Offering a return lower than the one expected for the investors' risk could only ever have led to stagnation, unfinished work, and legal arguments with rent seekers, which is what finally occurred.

In his doctoral thesis, Andrew Primmer demonstrated that the main reason behind Britain's low investment in Colombia's railways during the Belle-Époque, was the country's poor creditor performance, even by Latin American standards. In his thesis, the author elaborated on this point, explaining that there was no political consensus regarding the convenience of honouring external debt and improving Colombia's debtor records. As well as ignoring the *risk-return trade off* principle, the Colombian elite in the late nineteenth century was not convinced enough that they were competing for scarce resources, and the advantage of reducing its borrowing costs.

Some members of the Colombian elite had some notion of the *risk-return trade off* principle. In a communication from 1872 with the Ministry of Finance, Aquileo Parra, the Colombian Ambassador in London commented on the guaranties of 7% as follows:

> Under the present circumstances I attribute very little efficacy in guaranteeing a system of 7 per 100 over the capital that would have to be invested in the works covered by the law of 5th June.
>
> Firstly, the interest is not enough for the capital employed in a far and little known country, except for notoriety which gives us political turbulence. At the same time London can place funds that with the same risk produce such interest or one higher, as happens with the issuing of certain loans that offer a high interest, e.g., ones like Turkey, Paraguay, Honduras, and, some others which offer to pay even a ten per cent. (Parra, 1873, p. 72)

Colombia's bond reached its lowest yield in the nineteenth century, in 1874 with a rate of 8.8%. Such a value was the result of debt restructuring, and agreement with the bondholders in the same year, in what was convened to reducing the debt stock to £2 million. But even under such nadir, the borrowing costs were still higher than the one that could make a guarantee system of 7% to build the Northern railway workable. A feasible plan would have required a guarantee of at least 9%, but that was probably beyond the Colombian government's financial ability. In such a case, reducing the borrowing costs was probably the only feasible way to build long-distance lines.

The Colombian government only fulfilled their foreign debt payments up to 1879, which is what led to a new wave of its bond yields increasing in the last two decades of the nineteenth century. This was especially unfortunate, due to the fact that it was precisely during those years that the British overseas investment was in its apogee. Colombia was in a different situation to Argentina, and Chile and Mexico from 1888, as the country never managed to reduce its borrowing costs to reasonable levels.

Argentina, which funded a substantial proportion of its railway network with British capital, is an excellent example to contrast against Colombia's experience. After some initial disruptions, in 1862 the Argentine government adopted a guarantee system, which assured a minimum yearly return of 7% for capital invested up to £6000 per mile (Lewis, 1983, p. 10). One of the benefits of such a system was that it allowed the construction of three main lines, the Western Railway (Ferrocarril Oeaste), the Central Railway (Ferrocarril Central), and the Buenos Aires Great Southern Railway, around which a proper network could be built (Lewis, 1983, p. 16). The conditions for the Central Railway's building were even improved in 1873 as the government increased its maximum threshold of guaranteed capital return up to £6400, plus one league of land to each side of the line (Lewis, 1983, p. 16).

The importance of the three long-distance Argentine railways relies on the fact that they meet the conditions for a proper railway network with potential for further expansion, which actually occurred in the 1880s. This meant exploiting ***network externalities***, and actually integrating a significant part of the territory. The Argentine railways also faced their own problems, and the way forward for the government was far from easy. Such lines, however, met the fundamental conditions required for the adoption of steam technology, and to transform Argentina from a humble and remote country to one of the richest in the world in the early twentieth century. The economic change was so intense that it attracted thousands of European immigrants in search of prosperity.

The Argentina case evidences the benefits of lower borrowing costs and access to foreign investment. The guarantee system of 7% worked in this country because its borrowing costs were low enough to make such a return attractive. Without being able to fulfil such pre-conditions, it is not surprising that the same system did not work in Colombia, and the plans for the Colombian Northern railway were unrealistic.

If the plans for the Colombian railways construction were unrealistic in the 1870s, in the 1880s, they were to become delusional. In 1879, the Colombian bond yield started to skyrocket, reaching a peak in 1895 with a rate of 35.6%, a level that made any kind of foreign investment almost impossible. The bond yields declined transitorily between 1897 and 1900, but probably as a result of the One Thousand Day War (Guerra de los Mil Dias), they rose again before going back into decline in 1904.

In 1905, Colombian bond yields finally fell below 7% (5.5%), and for first time since 1825, the borrowing costs made large scale railway investment feasible. The actual fact is that an affordable borrowing cost is just a pre-condition, and in 1905 Colombia took only a step in the right direction. A railway project demands massive resources, detailed studies, and long gestation periods (Lewis, 1983). Colombia's main problem back then was that the window of opportunity that was the *Belle-Époque* only remained open for nine years more, up to July 1914, when the First World War commenced. The war changed the nature of international capital markets, and the once vast British financial resources were no longer available for foreign investment. The window to be a part of the first era of globalisation was over.

In 1905, Colombia filled the pre-condition that Chile had reached in 1842, Argentina in 1857, and Mexico in 1888, with a borrowing cost of lower than 7%. As those countries had integrated earlier into the world capital markets, they were able to attract vast sums of resources for their railways, which propelled their exports and potential GDP. In other words, Colombia missed the *Belle-Époque*.

Among the four countries analysed in this book, Argentina was the one which was more successful in attracting foreign capital. Figure 2.3 shows market capitalisation, which is the total market value of all of the companies from a country listed in the London Stock Market and the United States Stock Exchanges, for the period 1865–1914 for the four studied countries. Certainly, a high proportion of those companies were railways, which were integrated into international capital markets, and could therefore be funded by foreign capital.

Argentina was the country in Latin America that benefited the most from the possibilities of the *Belle-Époque*. The gap between its lower borrowing costs, the 7% guarantee system, plus *network externalities*, created the economic conditions for an authentic economic miracle. What is also important is that these conditions were fulfilled just in time to take advantage of the full *Belle-Époque*, and not partially as was the case for Mexico (after 1888), or marginally as was the case for Colombia (after 1905).

After examining Colombian bond yield fluctuations, a natural question that arises is: why did Colombian policy-makers not continue to reduce the country's borrowing costs after 1874? The answer leads us to examine the political economy behind the approach to the international capital

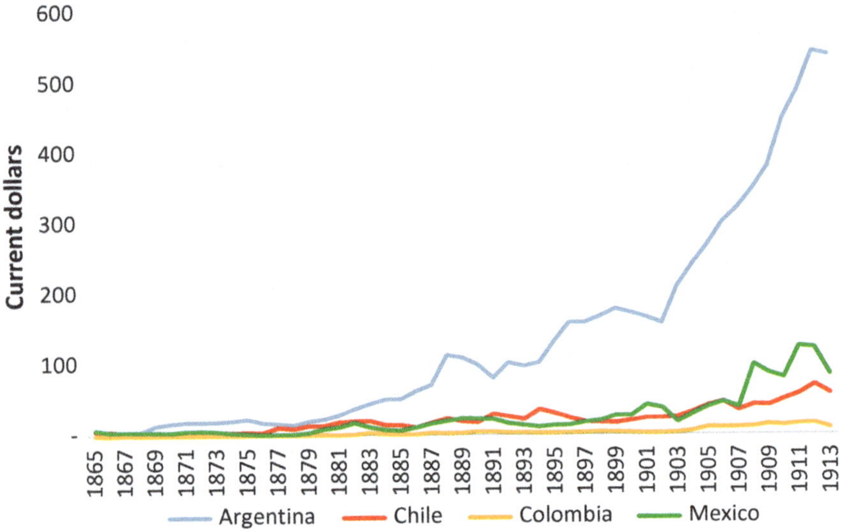

Fig. 2.3 Market capitalisation: companies listed in the London Stock Market and United States Stock Exchanges, 1865–1913 (Source: Global Financial Data Finaeon, n.d.)

market. The consolidation of a radical conservative rule, known as *La Regeneración* (The Regeneration) (1878–1904), established the centralised, ultra-catholic, and protectionism regime, which closed Colombia's opportunity for integration into the world economy.

2.4 The Political Economy of Belle-Époque in Colombia

During the railway era, Colombia passed through three very different political regimes: the radical Liberal-Federalist (1863–1878), *La Regenaracion* (1878–1904), and the Moderate Conservative Hegemony (1904–1930). The first and the second were very dogmatic in their ideologies and economic policies, which is what contributed to the political antagonism and the difficulty to reach a minimum political consensus, which has characterised Colombian political history.

The radical Liberals consolidated their rule with the 1863 constitution, although they were in power from the mid-nineteenth century. The 1863 constitution renamed the country the United States of Colombia, following an extreme federal regime and a liberal ideology inspired by Manchester Liberalism. Under this framework, the nine States of Colombia were united to perpetuity in a confederation, and each one had wide ranging autonomy in terms of taxes, regulation, and even their own armies. The laissez-faire doctrine was the very essence of the Liberal-Federalist era, which is why they advocated boosting free trade and Colombia's integration into the world economy.

The Liberal's agenda also included the establishment of secular education, and *desamortizacion* (confiscation of church land), which irremediably clashed with the interests of the Conservatives. The liberal government of General Mosquera issued a law on 9 September 1861, declaring the confiscation of Mortmain lands (Desamortizacion de Bienes de Manos Muertas) and Catholic Church loans (*Census*). The decree established that the religious communities' lands and loans would become property of the state in exchange for treasury bonds with an annual yield of 6% (Junguito, 2018). The measure was aimed not only at land redistribution and quicker circulation of these assets, but also as a practical way to cover government fiscal deficits (Junguito, 2018).

With the revenues from the sale of confiscated land and loans, the government planned to repurchase internal debt, for which it paid interest of between 18% and 25%. In this way, the government intended to replace an expensive internal debt, for a more affordable way of financing at 6%. In other words, the liberal government wanted to reduce its borrowing costs, which was essential in balancing its budget and eventually serving foreign debt.

Jaramillo and Meisel (2009) estimated that the government collected around \$9.3 million up to 1868 with the Confiscation of Mortmain Lands Law. Such resources certainly helped the government to cover its expenditure without additional fiscal pressure. Junguito (2010) estimates that the fiscal deficit between 1864 and 1870 accounted for around \$6 million, which was mainly covered by revenues coming from the sale of lands, and loans confiscated. In fact, the total public debt increased from \$43.7 million in 1861 to just \$45.2 million in 1870 (Junguito, 2018), which meant that the government could accommodate a substantial fiscal deficit without heavily relying on additional debt.

In addition, Jaramillo and Meisel (2009) concluded that the Confiscation of Mortmain Lands Law contributed to the early development of banking in Colombia, as it removed the main obstacle for the surge of the modern financial sector: the church's monopoly of credit with *Census* loans. Once such a pre-condition was fulfilled, it was followed by others of the Liberals' most prominent reforms: *Free Banking*. Under such framework, banks were allowed to issue their own paper money, convertible to gold, up to the point where it was supported by metal reserves. The Free Banking system has important benefits as it is flexible enough to provide liquidity, but the conversion to metals prevents inflation (White, 2016).

The Liberals' reforms were paving the way for an economic take-off. The establishment of the first banks in Colombia with the establishment of the Free Banking system was certainly a breakthrough in the way of progress, as an incipient credit market commenced to germinate. Likewise, the Confiscation of Mortmain Lands law helped the liberal regime to balance their budgets, and left the government in a suitable position to look for an agreement with international bondholders, which finally occurred in 1873.[6]

In 1874, Colombian bond yield (8.8%) was at its lowest since 1824 as a result of the Liberals' endeavour to improve Colombia's fiscal situation, and the agreement reached on 18 December 1873 with the bondholders in London. The prospect of railway construction under a guarantee system of 7% began to look complex, but very close to becoming feasible in the near future. The government's borrowing costs were approaching the magic level of making the railways project attractive enough to foreign investors.

Why did the Colombian government not persevere in trying to reduce its borrowing costs? The most probable answer is the civil war of 1876, which was a result of an escalation in the conflict between the liberal government, the church and the Conservative party. Such a conflict consumed a significant share of government resources, which was a constraint to the continued improvement of Colombia's foreign debt profile.

The feeling about the impact of the civil war was evident in the memoirs of Nicolas Esguerra from the Ministry of Finances in 1876, who commented on the progress of the civil works and made the following statement:

> Much more could have been done without the shock given to our credit with the last, and unjustifiable revolution, and without the defalcation that it caused to public revenue: but the little that was done is a measurement of what could be achieved if peace prevails. (Esguerra, 1876, p. 72)

[6] Memoria del Secretario de Hacienda 1875 Nicolas Esguerra (Pages XLVII).

According to Junguito (2018), the three Ministries of Finance between 1876 and 1878, commented consistently on the negative impact of the war not just on government finances, but also on international trade and foreign debt. In fact, from the Ministry of Finances in 1878, J.M. Quijano described in his memoirs how government resources became exhausted in 1876 due to violence which started in the country in late 1875. In fact, J.M. Quijano maintained that the war made a new foreign loan fail (Junguito, 2018), which certainly had the potential to improve Colombia's debt record.

Prominent historians (Busnell, 1993; Safford & Palacios, 2002) put forward the notion that secular education implemented by the Liberals was the main factor behind the 1876 civil war, but it was probably the election of President Aquileo Parra for the period of 1876–1878 that triggered the actions. Such a movement was seen as an unacceptable threat to conservative values and the Catholic Church, one of the country's more powerful institutions, which ended in a violent confrontation. It is not surprising that the rebellion against the liberal government began in the west, in the conservative state of Cauca, which was close to Antioquia, the most conservative of states in the Colombian Union in the nineteenth century.

In 1880, the liberal period came to an end with the victory of Rafael Nuñez, who would establish an extreme conservative and centralist regime known as 'The Regeneration' (*La Regeneración*). One of his first government terms in 1880–1882, Nuñez started to increase national executive power over the states and his protectionism agenda by raising tariffs (Busnell, 1993). Nuñez won the presidency again in 1885 for a further period of two years, to which a liberal revolt broke out as they feared substantial changes to the 1863 constitution (Busnell, 1993). Such rebellion was supressed with support coming from the Conservatives, and moved the president to abolish the 1863 constitution, formally ending the liberal-federal era in Colombia.

The new conservative regime consolidated its power with the 1886 constitution, which remained as the Colombia *Carta Magna* until 1991, and it changed the name from the United States of Colombia to the current Republic of Colombia. The constitution was largely influenced by Miguel Antonio Caro, a radical conservative politician, who would become Colombia's president between 1894 and 1898 but, as vice president, he acted as the country's highest authority from 1892 due to President Nuñez's illness (Junguito, 2018).

The Regeneration's economic program reversed many of the Liberal's reforms, but there were two measurements related to the development of finance in Colombia of an especially high relevance. They both strongly affected the entire economy, and delayed the Colombian economic take-off up to the 1910s. The first of such policies was the suspension of payments for external debt, which came to an end in 1879 with the end of the Liberal's regime. The government did not look for an agreement with foreign bondholders until 1895, when the bond yield was at 31.6%, a level substantially higher than the 10.8% observed in 1879.

The agreement reached in 1895 was very favourable for Colombia, as it reduced the stock of external debt from £3.5 million to £2.7 million as well as a reduction in the interest rate to 1.5% from 4.5% in the 1873 agreement (Junguito, 2018). The government concluded the debt conversion in 1898, but only served the payments for a few months due to the uprising of the One Thousand Days War, the most intense and final civil war between the Liberals and Conservatives.

The new debt payment suspension lasted up until 1905, when the government signed a new agreement with foreign bondholders, known as the *Holguin-Avebury Treaty*, which essentially ratified commitments from 1895. With the new agreement, the bond yields finally declined to levels lower than 7% and, for first time, the guarantee system for railway construction had some possibility of being viable. The actual fact was that the lower borrowing costs were only a step in the right direction, and Colombia only fulfilled all the pre-conditions for railway construction in the 1920s. The *Holguin-Avebury Treaty* was reached under a new political regime, which replaced The Regeneration and lasted up until 1930, which was known as the Moderate Conservative Hegemony. Such political rule, if still conservative, was significantly more moderate than The Regeneration, and took a more pragmatic approach towards its relationships with the liberal opposition and foreign creditors.

The enormous borrowing costs during The Regeneration made any attempt to build public infrastructure financially impossible. No public work was profitable enough to survive the high rates of the Colombian bond yields. The payments of the external debt were, however, only one of the economic setbacks caused by The Regeneration rule. This regime also induced monetary and credit instability which had a significant effect on Colombia's financial development.

The Liberals replaced the colonial credit system, based on the monopoly of the Ecclesiastical Loans (*Census*), for a Free Banking system. Such a framework operated formally from 1871 until 1886, but in 1880, President Rafael Nuñez established the National Bank (Banco Nacional), and in 1885, granted it the monopoly for issuing bank notes whose face value had to be accepted, and this ended convertibility (Kalmanovitz, 2017).

The civil war of 1885 led to a large fiscal deficit, but the government could now fund itself by the National Bank's emission, which inevitably led to a period of enormous inflation for first time in Colombian history (Kalmanovitz, 2017). The National Bank, finally came to an end in 1896, after a congress survey discovered illegal issuing emissions from 1889 to repay government debt (Junguito, 2018). Despite the National Bank being officially closed, the government continued issuing notes in order to fund the One Thousand Days War, which led to hyperinflation rates of around 400% in 1900, and 330% in 1902 (Kalmanovitz, 2017). The Regeneration's economic programme seriously affected the banking system. It is worth noting that only 12 banks, from 42 in 1886, survived the One Thousand Days War, and the operation of the National Bank (Kalmanovitz, 2017).

In 1905, the Moderate Conservative regime introduced several reforms with the purpose of resuming the gold standard, abandoned since 1886 (Meisel, 1992). Such measures were oriented towards currency devaluation in order to reach the parity of gold, and agreement with some private banks to issue bank notes. In 1909, the government restricted the banking system even more, and prohibited any issuing of bank notes. Between 1909 and 1923 (when the Colombian Central Bank was established), the financial system returned to the colonial framework where circulating could be only issued by the minting of gold and silver. Such a system was effective in reducing inflation, but it was a major constraint for the development of a modern financial sector, capable of funding credit and boosting economic growth.

The triumph of The Regeneration meant the reversal of a series of economic policies put forward by the Liberals, which could meet the preconditions for the development of a modern financial sector, and the integration of Colombia into the world economy, by capital inflows and trade expansion. Such a watershed limited Colombia's capacity to fund the construction of the railways and the embracement of steam technology. Despite some of The Regeneration's policies being fixed in 1905 with the arrival of the Moderate Conservative regime, such measures were not enough to produce an economic take-off. During the onset of the First World War, railway construction in Colombia was still a 'pending task'.

References

Busnell, D. (1993). *The Making of Modern Colombia: A Nation in Spite of Itself.* Berkeley and Los Angeles: University of California Press.

Cisneros, F. (1878). *Report on the Project to Construct a Railway from the Bay of Buenaventura, upon the Pacific Ocean, and the River Cauca.* New York: D. Van Nostrand.

Correa, J. (2012). *De Buenaventura al Caribe: el ferrocarril del pacífico y la conexión interoceánica (1872–2012).* Cali: Colegio de Estudios Superiores de Administración-CESA.

Department of Commerce of the United States. (1924). *Colombia Commerce and Industries 1922 and 1923. The Trade Information Bulletin No. 223*, Latin America Division.

Esguerra, N. (1876 [2016]). Memoria del Secretario de Hacienda I Fomento Dirijida al Presidente de la República para el Congreso de 1876. In A. Meisel & M. Ramirez (Eds.), *Memorias de Hacienda y del Tesoro.* Bogota: Banco de la República.

Global Financial Data Finaeon. (n.d.). *Global Financial Data Database and Indices.* Retrieved from http://www.globalfinancialdata.com/

Herranz-Loncan, A. (2011). *The Contribution of Railways to Economic Growth in Latin America before 1914: A Growth Accounting Approach.* MPRA Paper No. 33578.

Jaramillo, R., & Meisel, A. (2009). Más allá de la retórica de la reacción. Análisis económico de la desamortización en Colombia, 1861–1888. *Revista de Economía Institucional, 11*, 45–81.

Junguito, R. (2010). Las Finanzas Públicas en el Siglo XIX. In A. Meisel & M. Ramirez (Eds.), *Economía Colombiana del SIglo XIX.* Bogota: Fondo de Cultura Económica.

Junguito, R. (2018). *Cien Episodios de la Historia Económica de Colombia.* Bogota: Ariel.

Kalmanovitz, S. (2017). *Nueva Historia Económica de Colombia.* Bogota: Universidad Jorge Tadeo Lozano.

Lewis, C. (1983 [2015]). *British Railways in Argentina, 1857–1914: A Case Study of Foreign Investment.* New York, NY: Bloomsbury Academic.

Lewis, C. (2002). *Argentina: A Short History.* Oxford: Oneworld Publications.

Maddison Project Database, Version 2018. Bolt, Jutta, Robert Inklaar, Herman de Jong and Jan Luiten van Zanden. (2018). *Rebasing 'Maddison': New Income Comparisons and the Shape of Long-Run Economic Development.* Retrieved from https://www.rug.nl/ggdc/historicaldevelopment/maddison/releases/maddison-project-database-2018

Marichal, C. (2014). *Historia mínima de la deuda externa de Latinoamérica, 1820–2010.* Mexico D.F.: El Colegio de México.

McGreevy, W. (1971). *An Economic History of Colombia, 1845–1930* (Latin America Studies Series). Cambridge: The University Press.

Meisel, A. (1992). Free Banking in Colombia. In K. Dowd (Ed.), *The Experience of Free Banking*. London and New York: Routledge.

Meisel, A., Ramirez, M. T., & Jaramillo, J. (2014). Muy tarde pero rentables: Los ferrocarriles en Colombia durante el periodo 1920–1950. *Cuadernos de Historia Económica y Empresarial*, No. 34.

Melo, J. (2015). Las Vicisitudes del Modelo Liberal (1850–1899). In J. Ocampo (Ed.), *Historia Económica De Colombia* (4th ed.). Bogota: Fondo de Cultura Economica/Fedesarrollo.

MOxLAD. (n.d.). *Montevideo-Oxford Latin America Economic History Database*. Retrieved from http://moxlad.cienciassociales.edu.uy/

Pachon, A., & Ramirez, M. T. (2006). *La Infraestructura de Transporte en Colombia Durante el Siglo XX*. Bogota: Fondo de Cultura Económica/Banco de la República.

Parra, A. (1873). Memoria del Secretario de Hacienda I Fomento Dirijida al Presidente de la República para el Congreso de 1873. In A. Meisel & M. Ramirez (Eds.), *Memorias de Hacienda y del Tesoro*. Bogota: Banco de la República.

Poor, H. (1889). *Poor's Manual of the Railroads of the United States*. New York: Poor's Publication Co.

Safford, F., & Palacios, M. (2002). *Colombia Fragmented Land, Divided Society* (Latin American Histories). New York: Oxford University Press.

Summerhill, W. (2000). *Profit and Productivity on Argentine Railroads, 1857–1913*. Los Angeles: Department of History, UCLA (Mimeo).

Summerhill, W. (2003). *Order Against Progress. Government, Foreign Investment, and Railroads in Brazil, 1854–1913*. Stanford: Stanford University Press.

White, L. (2016). Introduction. In J. Couyoumdjian (Ed.), *Economía sin Banco Central. La Banca Libre en Chile (1860–1898)*. Santiago: Empresa El Mercurio S.A.P.

CHAPTER 3

The Take-off, 1914–1929: Coffee, Railways, and Regional Divergence

Abstract After a long period of stagnation during the *Belle-Époque* (1870–1914), Colombia finally experienced an economic take-off early in the twentieth century. The fundamental question in this chapter is: ***what was the reason behind Colombia's economic take-off late in the decade of the 1910s, and its consolidation in the 1920s?***

Colombia's economic take-off was export-driven or, more accurately, a coffee-driven one. That was a result of Colombia resuming its access to the international capital market, which allowed it to build up a precarious, but workable, transport infrastructure in the 1910s. Such an infrastructure expanded and consolidated in the 1920s, and Colombia could for the first time integrate the farming areas of the inlands with the ports on the coast in a way that incorporated steam technology.

Keywords Economic take-off • Export-led growth • Coffee • Railways • Steam navigation • The Antioquia railway • External debt

After a long period of stagnation during the *Belle-Époque* (1870–1914), Colombia finally experienced an economic take-off early in the twentieth century. Such prosperity was export-driven, based on coffee cultivation in the west of the country which was mainly untouched by the War of a Thousand Days (1899–1903), the most devastating civil war in Colombian

I. Luzardo-Luna, *Colombia's Slow Economic Growth*,
Palgrave Studies in Economic History,
https://doi.org/10.1007/978-3-030-25755-2_3

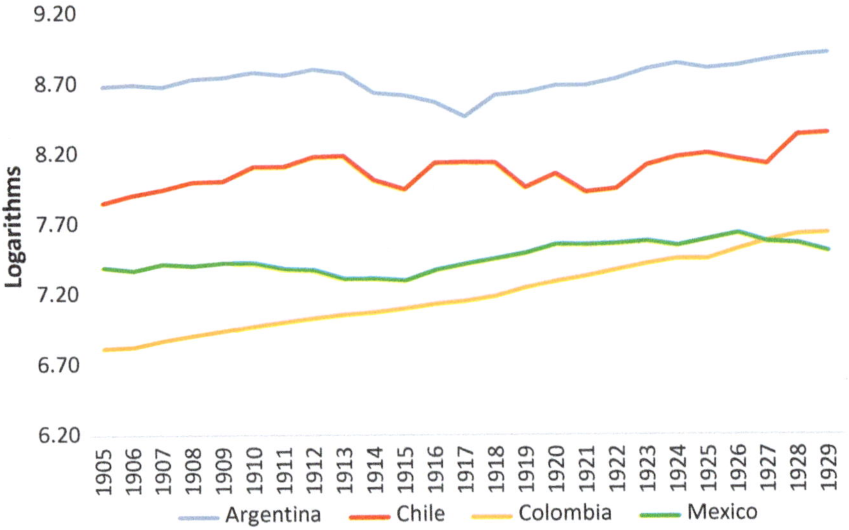

Fig. 3.1 Real GDP per capita at 2011 USD prices (logs), 1905–1929 (Source: Maddison Project Database, Version 2018. Bolt, Jutta, Robert Inklaar, Herman de Jong and Jan Luiten van Zanden (2018))

history (Bejarano, 2015). Despite the intensity of the war, in the years that followed the end of hostilities, Colombia finally moved in a positive direction to achieve sustained economic growth and enjoyed one of the most prosperous and peaceful periods in its history.

From 1907, GDP per capita began to grow in a sustained way, but it was after the First World War that the economy's growth rate accelerated significantly enough to induce a decisive economic transformation. It was in the late 1910s that Colombia saw its economic take-off, and in the 1920s, the country reached its greatest economic growth rate in history, consolidating its transition to a modern economy.

If it is necessary to define a particular year for Colombia's economic take-off, 1919 would be a good choice. During this year, the real GDP per capita rose by 6.2%, a rate never seen before in Colombian history, driven by a significant increase in coffee exports. Figure 3.1 presents the GDP per capita in natural logarithms[1] for the period 1905–1929. Postwar economic growth was so intense that Colombia significantly reduced its gap between

[1] Series are presented in logarithms in order to reduce their volatility and to make it easier to track long-term trends.

Table 3.1 Constant average real GDP per capita growth rates, 1909–1928

Period	*Argentina (%)*	*Chile (%)*	*Colombia (%)*	*Mexico (%)*
1909–1918	−0.90	1.80	2.80	0.50
1919–1928	2.90	2.70	4.50	1.10

Source: Maddison Project Database, Version 2018. Bolt, Jutta, Robert Inklaar, Herman de Jong and Jan Luiten van Zanden (2018)

Argentina and Chile, and in 1927, it even overtook Mexico. In fact, between 1909 and 1929, Colombia enjoyed the highest growth rate out of the four countries studied in this book, as is presented in Table 3.1. If the economy showed good performance between 1909 and 1919, it was in the 1920s that Colombia's economic growth went through its golden age.

Colombia's good economic performance in the early twentieth century was shaped by a characteristic that persists up to the present day: the absence of any major economic depressions. Argentina and Chile were heavily affected by the disruption of economic order caused by the First World War, as these economies were strongly integrated into the world economy. Similarly, Mexico saw two major economic depressions with the Mexican Revolution (1910–1917) and the Cristero War (1926–1929).

The fundamental question in this chapter is: *what was the reason behind Colombia's economic take-off late in the decade of the 1910s, and its consolidation in the 1920s?* The immediate cause was that the country moved into an export-led growth model, similar to that followed by Argentina, Chile, and Mexico, during the Belle-Époque, but based on coffee exports. Such a commodity would change Colombia's economic history, due to it being the first time the country had a product to export on a large scale, generating spill-overs for the rest of the economy. Figure 3.2 shows the exports' share of GDP between 1905 and 1939. Exports were gaining ground in Colombia's economy from the 1900s, but they accelerated in the 1910s. The great leap, however, was yet to come in 1919, when exports reached a share of 18.4%, which is what led to the substantial increase in GDP per capita.

Colombia's economic take-off was export-driven or, more accurately, a coffee-driven one. Figure 3.3 shows coffee exports (in 60 kg bags), for the period 1905–1939. In the 1910s, coffee exports started to increase significantly, and by 1913, Colombia overtook the symbolic threshold of one million bags, before reaching the 1919 and 1921 boom periods. Coffee exports accelerated further in the 1920s, and in the first half of this decade they reached their highest pace of growth in terms of volume. It is

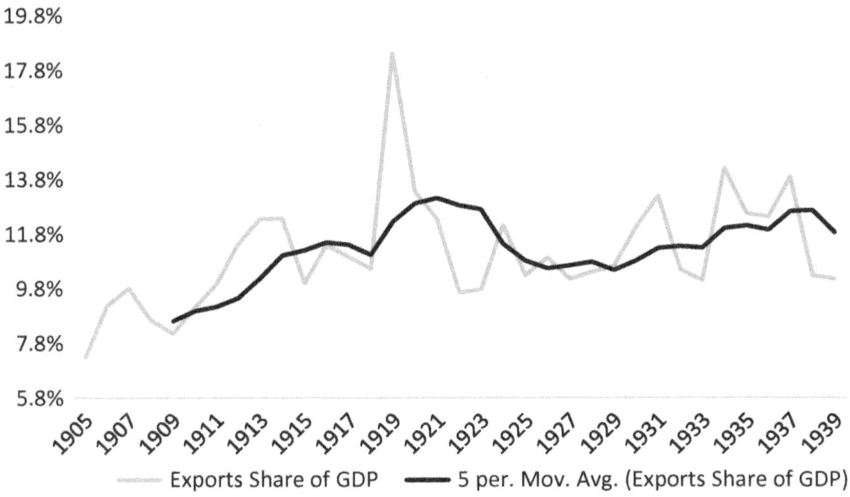

Fig. 3.2 Exports' share of GDP, 1905–1939 (%) (Source: Urrutia, Pontón, & Posada, 2002)

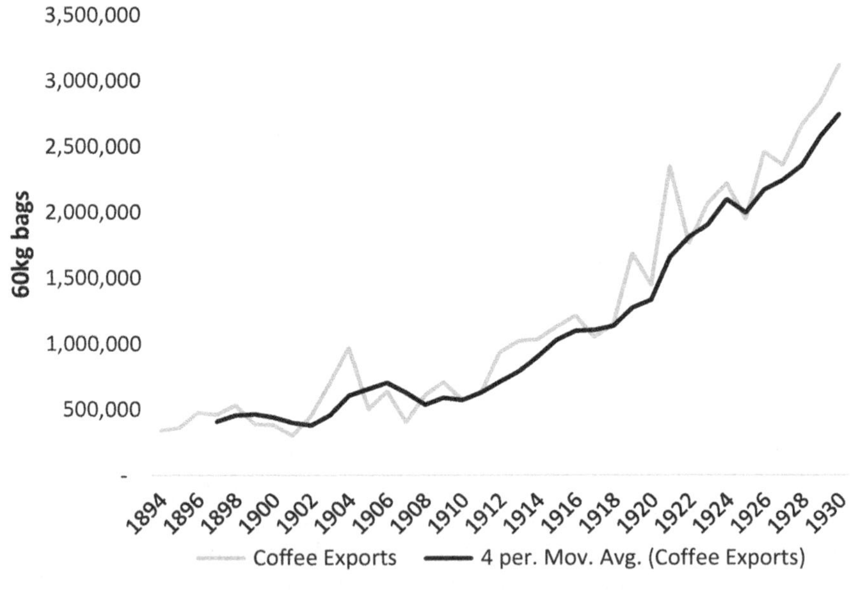

Fig. 3.3 Coffee exports, 1894–1930 (in 60 kg bags) (Source: Urrutia et al., 2002)

worth noting that in 1924, almost 80% of Colombian export was coffee, which reinforced the hypothesis that the export boom in the early twentieth century was essentially due to a boom in coffee exportation.

After noting the importance of coffee in Colombia's take-off, some questions emerge, such as *what was the driving force behind the coffee exports growth? Why did coffee exports only start to accelerate in the 1910s? Why did the coffee boom only occur in the 1920s?*

A potential answer in addressing the first question is the international price of coffee. If they were exceptionally high in that period, Colombian farmers and exporters were only reacting to an opportunity to generate profit. Figure 3.4 shows the monthly closing wholesale price of coffee traded in the New York commodities market between 1890 and 1939. Coffee was traded for a very high price in the 1890s, similar to that

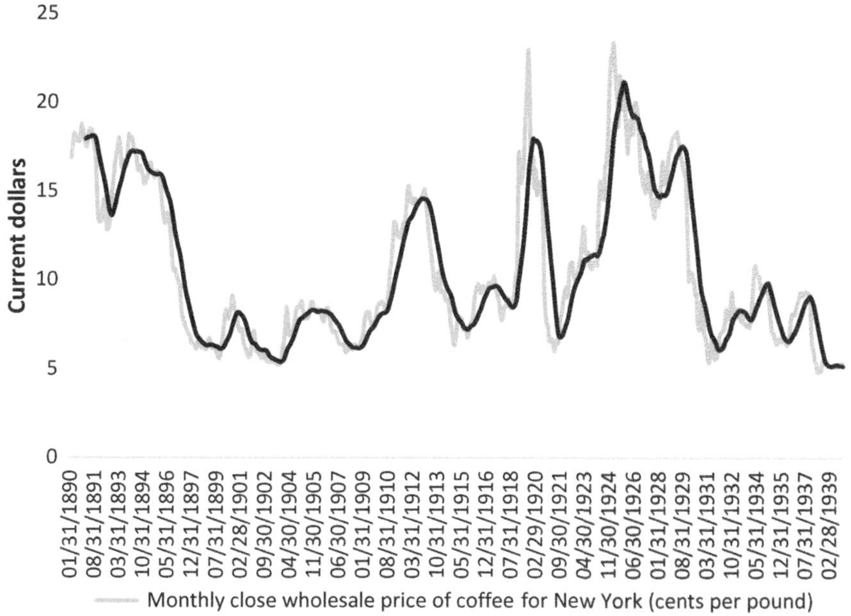

Fig. 3.4 Monthly closing wholesale price of coffee traded in the New York commodities market, January 1890–December 1939 (Source: Global Financial Data Finaeon, n.d.)

observed in the second half of the 1920s when Colombia's economic growth rate was in its apogee. The actual fact is that when coffee exports in volume terms began to accelerate in the late 1910s, the international coffee price was not particularly high, which indicates that an acceleration in exports was due to supply-side factors. If the price of coffee in New York increased between 1910 and 1912, it went into decline from early 1913 to late 1918. Despite the depressed prices, the volume of Colombian exported coffee bags increased steadily between 1913 and 1917, which evidences that there was a structural change in the country's production capacity. This is also in line with the fact that when the international price of coffee declined after 1929 and remained low for the entire decade of the 1930s, the volume of exports continued increasing. Something was different during the interwar period compared to the Belle-Époque, which is what made exporting coffee profitable, even with unfavourable international prices. This fact suggests a substantial reduction in coffee production costs.

In the 1910s, coffee production costs, largely influenced by transportation costs, were very probably significantly lower than in the 1890s, as they allowed exporters to make a profit even with a substantially lower international price. This fact, led to the structural cause of Colombia's economic take-off; the railways expansion, which allowed the country to partially overcome its geographical isolation. Such an accomplishment meant a transportation revolution, which finally incorporated steam technology on a large scale into Colombia's production function and led to a substantial reduction in costs. After several decades of stagnation in the late nineteenth century, Colombia could finally construct a reasonable number of railway kilometres, and this is what made the export-led growth model feasible. After all of the delays it suffered, Colombia finally could embrace the general purpose technology of the industrial revolution.

3.1 The Antioquia Railway and the Take-off in the Late 1910s

Colombia could not experience an economic take-off in the 1890s because it did not have the minimum of transport infrastructure to boost its exports, and take advantage of high international coffee prices of that time. Such a situation changed in the early twentieth century, when the country finally saw a significant increase in terms of railway kilometres, especially in medium-distance lines over one hundred kilometres.

Figure 3.5 presents the number of open railway kilometres and the volume of coffee exports, in terms of the number bags, for the period of 1905–1929. The correlation between the two variables is 92%, indicating a strong association.

An observer may put forward the situation of reverse causality, in which the railway network itself did not lead to a substantial increase in coffee exports, but on the contrary, the export boom allowed the country to harvest enough resources to fund railway construction. Such a hypothesis, even if plausible, is unlikely. As Melo (2015) shows, there was a significant increase in coffee production in the 1890s. The only railway line, however, which could be completed in this decade was the Cartagena-Calamar line in the north of the country. The actual fact is that the Colombian economy did not take off in the 1890s, but did so in the late 1910s when the international coffee prices were not particularly high, which is why the 1910s' surge was very probably a supply-driven boom. What was different then than in the late nineteenth century, was that now the country had a minimal transport infrastructure that permitted coffee exports with reasonable freight costs.

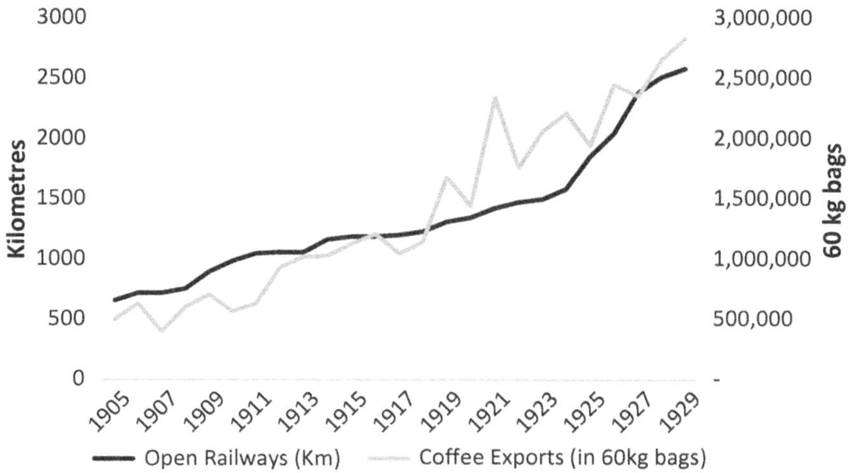

Fig. 3.5 Coffee exports and open railways, 1905–1929 (Source: For coffee exports: Urrutia et al., 2002. For open railway kilometres: Pachon & Ramirez, 2006)

What made Colombia's export capacity in the 1910s different from the 1890s was not just more kilometres of railways, but also the nature of these lines, which allowed the integration of the coffee cultivating regions inland with the ports on the Caribbean Sea. Even though Colombia's railways were far from being a 'network' in 1914, the country completed several medium-distance lines such as the Antioquia railway-AR, the Girardot railway-GR, and La Dorada railway extension, which linked the inland areas with the Magdalena River, through which the coffee freight could reach the port of Barranquilla. Of all the new railways, the most important was by far the Antioquia railway, which was a fundamental instrument in Colombia's economic take-off.

As has been noted by several scholars (Meisel, Ramirez, & Jaramillo, 2014; Pachon & Ramirez, 2006), the railways were complementary to steam navigation on the Magdalena River. The increase in the railways' freight capacity in the 1910s also meant an increase in fluvial freight (Pachon & Ramirez, 2006). Most of the freight in Colombia was carried on the Magdalena River, where all the main fluvial ports were located at that time, except Puerto Mallarino on the Cauca River, which accounted for approximately just 5% of the received freight between 1915 and 1919.[2] The increase in fluvial traffic in the early twentieth century, which rose to 259,000 tonnes from 181,000 in 1915, was essentially down to an increase in navigation along the Magdalena River.

The integration of the three means of transportation—the new medium-distance railways, steam navigation along the Magdalena River, and Barranquilla Port on the Atlantic Ocean—was the key infrastructure which made coffee exportation take place on as large a scale. As steam navigation and the Barranquilla's port were operatives since the late nineteenth century, what was different were the railways, particularly the Antioquia railway.

Figure 3.6 presents rail freight moved and coffee exports. A significant share of the coffee exports which propelled Colombia's take-off were carried on the Magdalena River in the 1910s by the recently inaugurated railway lines. In this notable period of growth, the Antioquia railway played a critical role. This line increased its share of total freight carried on railways from 4.4% in 1910 to 12.9% in 1919, in the context where other lines also saw significant increases in freight transportation. It is worth noting that the railway that carried the largest quantity of freight, in terms

[2] Estimation based on data presented by Pachon and Ramirez (2006, pp. 85–87).

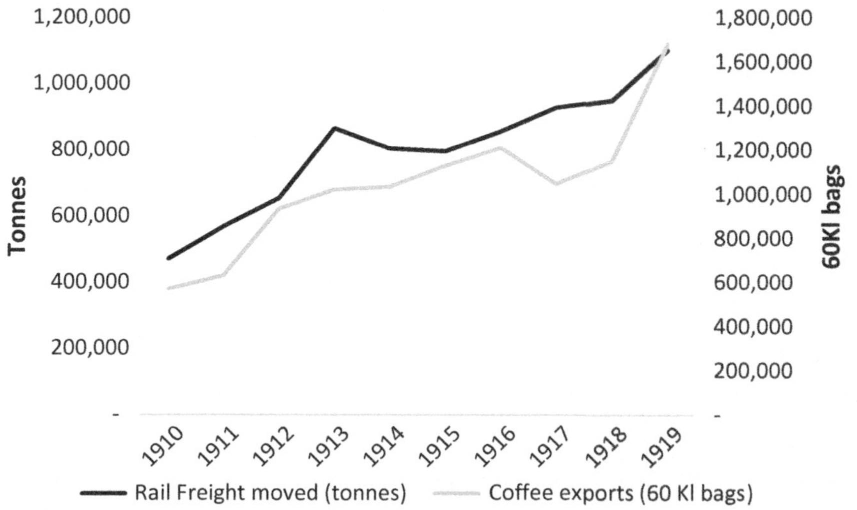

Fig. 3.6 Rail freight moved and coffee exports, 1910–1919 (Source: For rail freight moved: 1910–1917: Anuario General de Estadística de Colombia: 1918–1919: Pachon & Ramirez, 2006. For coffee exports: Urrutia et al., 2002)

of kilograms, in the 1910s, was the Santa Marta railway.[3] However, the kind of freight transported by this railway line was mainly bananas, and not coffee.

Clearly, a significant share of the new coffee exports was carried by the Antioquia Railway, which moved coffee bags from the inlands of Antioquia's mountains up to Puerto Berrio on the Magdalena River. Once there, the coffee bags continued their journey up to the ports of Barranquilla or Cartagena. Puerto Berrio was located lower down the Magdalena River than Girardot, where the Girardot railway terminated which served Cundinamarca, in a part of Bogota's influential area. Puerto Berrio's location had an important advantage over that of Girardot's, due to it being closer to the coast, and this meant lower transportation costs. According to the *Anuario Estadístico* (Statistical Yearbook) of 1915, the price of coffee was lower in Antioquia (COP$ 0.14 per kilogram) than in Cundinamarca and the north of Santander (COP$ 0.16 and COP$ 0.2

[3] The Santa Marta railway transported the 26.6% of total freight in 1910 and 15.1% in 1919 (Anuarios estadísticos, Departamento de Contraloría).

Table 3.2 Coffee production by region, 1898–1925 (thousands of 60 kg bags)

Departments	*1898*	*1913*	*1925*
Antioquia	70	185	415
Viejo Caldas	20	199	495
Cundinamarca	204	200	312
Santander (Including North of Santander)	270	305	331
Others	46	173	263
Total	610	1062	1816

Source: Ocampo (2015)

per kilogram, respectively). These regions were where concentrated coffee cultivation took place in the late nineteenth century but were poorly served by railways.

The Antioquia railway was the notable difference between the 1890s and 1910s. With the building and extension of this railway, Colombia finally overtook, although in a very precarious way, its chronic geographical insolation which made economic take-off unfeasible in the nineteenth century. The importance of Antioquia railway also could be noted for in the increase in coffee production in this region, which along with Caldas, was substantially higher than the levels observed in the rest of the country. Table 3.2 presents coffee production by region in Colombia for 1898, 1913, and 1925. While in 1898, Antioquia only accounted for the 11.5% of Colombia's coffee production, in 1925 it reached a level of 22.9%. The opposite was observed in Cundinamarca, which saw a decline in its share to 17.2% in 1925, substantially lower than the 33.4% observed in 1898.

As impressive as Antioquia is, so is the case for Caldas, which increased its share in coffee production from a marginal 3.3% to 18.7% in 1913, and to 27.3% in 1925. On the other hand, the case for Santander is similar to Cundinamarca in the sense that it lost its substantial share of coffee production between 1898 and 1925, although the region increased production in actual terms. Certainly, the two regions in the west, Antioquia and Caldas, were the actual drivers behind Colombia's economic take-off, while the regions in the east did not progress at the same pace. In other words, Colombia's economic progress that occurred in the 1910s had as its core the west of the country, and not the east, which cornered 77.7% of coffee production in 1898. Colombia's economic take-off was to a large extent, due to western Colombia's take-off.

Table 3.3 Coffee exports by the ports of Barranquilla, Cartagena, and Buenaventura, 1969–1929 (thousands of 60 kg bags)

Year	*Barranquilla*	*Cartagena*	*Buenaventura*
1916	44,948	9159	8698
1919	50,575	18,825	14,758
1921	68,897	21,493	33,433
1923	71,767	10,439	31,061
1927	70,950	19,551	41,980
1929	61,596	31,795	59,771

Source: Pachon and Ramirez (2006)

Western Colombia's good fortune was deeply integrated to the north coast of the country, especially to Barranquilla. This city was the main Atlantic Ocean port in the early twentieth century. As can be observed in Table 3.3, most of the coffee exports in the late 1910s, particularly in 1919, were exported from Barranquilla, although Buenaventura, on the Pacific Ocean, started to gain ground.

The transport infrastructure that enabled Colombia's transition to a modern economy (the Antioquia railway—Steam navigation on the Magdalena River—Port of Barranquilla) was still very precarious when compared to the standards observed in other industrial nations at that time. However, Colombia could for the first time integrate the farming areas of the inlands with the ports on the coast in a way that incorporated steam technology. Such infrastructure expanded and consolidated in the 1920s, which allowed for higher economic growth. Likewise, the new investments concentrated heavily in the west of the country, which ultimately moved the centre of gravity for Colombia's economy from the Magdalena River towards the Pacific Ocean via the port of Buenaventura.

3.2 The Take-off Consolidation in the 1920s and Regional Divergence

Colombia's economic take-off occurred in the late 1910s, but it was in 1920s that it became consolidated, and the country definitely moved into a new plateau of development. Colombia continued under the export-led growth model, and coffee continued to propel the country's prosperity. The 1919 coffee export boom was quickly overtaken by a larger boom in 1921, which in turn was significantly smaller than the 1926 and 1930s export volumes. The rate of economic growth was substantially higher than that observed in the late 1910s (see Table 3.1), and the country achieved qualitative accomplishments such as the founding of the Central Bank (Banco de la República), and the Financial Regulatory Agency (Superintendencia Financiera de Colombia) in 1923.

Colombia was on a high-speed road to economic development in the 1920s, and the country saw another decade of similar fortune in the 2000s. There were two immediate reasons behind such intense prosperity: high international coffee prices (see Fig. 3.4) and the acceleration in railway construction, especially in the west of the country. This latter was largely due to the significant resources that the Colombian government received from the United States as reparation for Panama's independence in 1903.

Panama's reparation accounted for 25.5 million dollars, around 4% of Colombia's GDP in 1925 (Pachon & Ramirez, 2006, p. 22). The United States paid Colombia the first 5 million in the second half of 1922, and both governments agreed on annual payments of the same amount up to 1926. 64.2% of those resources was invested in railways, which meant a substantial transformation in Colombia's infrastructure, which consolidated its economic take-off initiated in the late 1910s. To Panama's reparation, a massive increase in foreign loans was added, as international capital was attracted by institutional reforms, such as the foundation of the Central Bank and coffee exports (Meisel et al., 2014).

Table 3.4 Main Colombian railways by working kilometres, 1890–1929

Years	*Railways that served ports on the Magdalena River in the 1910s*			*Railways serving the Buenaventura Port in 1923*		*North (1)*	*North (2)*	*Others*
	Antioquia	*Girardot*	*La Dorada*	*Pacifico*	*Caldas*			
1890	48	31	29	52	–	–	–	123
1905	66	49	33	43	–	–	47	423
1910	102	132	111	94	–	12	62	475
1919	223	132	111	233	10	20	62	521
1923	242	132	111	330	50	27	62	546
1927	259	132	111	577	117	72	154	965
1929	320	132	111	577	117	90	172	1067

Source: Meisel et al. (2014)

In the 1920s, coffee exports continued to expand as a consequence of the international price recovery, but this was also fuelled by the expanding railways network. As in the late 1910s, coffee continued to be exported mainly through Barranquilla port, which was supplied by freight moved along the Magdalena River, which in turn was supplied by the Antioquia, La Dorada and the Girardot railways. As is shown in Table 3.3, however, Buenaventura gradually became more important throughout the 1920s, overtaking Cartagena in 1921, and converging with Barranquilla in 1929.

The rise of Buenaventura was a result of the high level of government investment in the construction of the Pacific railways which supplied the port. As Table 3.4 shows, these two railways underwent substantial expansion between 1919 and 1927, which was more substantial than that observed for the railways that served the fluvial ports on the Magdalena River. The major increase in open railways in the early 1920s occurred with the Pacific railway, which reached a length of 330 kilometres in 1923, from 233 in 1919. Also, in 1923, the Caldas railway was connected with the Pacific railway, integrating the coffee cultivating areas of Caldas with Buenaventura.

The government's massive investment in the Pacific railway, led to a gradual replacement of the Antioquia-Magdalena River-Barranquilla route, which was the core of Colombia's economic take-off in the late 1910s. Table 3.5 presents the accumulated investment in railways between 1924 and 1933. 40% of the accumulated investment in that period, and therefore Panama's indemnity, went into only one railway: the Pacific railway. This line increased its length to 577 kilometres in 1927, and remained growing, even during the Great Depression, up to an extension of 678 kilometres in 1933.

The number of open railway kilometres increased significantly in the west, linking the coffee cultivation areas in Viejo Caldas with Buenaventura port, which consolidated as the largest in terms of moving freight early in 1933. The difference between the east and the west in transportation infrastructure laid not only in the number of open railways, but also in the access of these railways to seaports, which is a fundamental reason behind the economic take-off being concentrated in the western part of Colombia.

The divide between the east and the west with respect to growth of coffee cultivation has been noted by several scholars (Bejarano, 2015; McGreevy, 1971; Ocampo, 2015). A common thesis for this anomaly is that the plantation size in the west was on average smaller than in the east, which led to an institutional difference in labour relationships (Bejarano,

Table 3.5 Accumulated investment in railways (millions of $USD), 1924–1933

Railway	*1924*	*1926*	*1928*	*1930*	*1933*	*Share 1933*
Pacifico	24.9	34.1	44.4	45	62.5	40.10%
Girardot	7.7	8.6	11	11.4	13.7	8.80%
Tolima	4.3	6	7.1	7.2	8.6	5.50%
Norte Sec. 1	3	9.1	12.6	12.8	15.4	9.90%
Norte Sec. 2		0.9	5.3	6.3	7.6	4.90%
Antioquia	2.2	4.5	6.1	6.9	8.9	5.70%
Caldas	0.7	1.3	1.3	1.3	1.6	1.00%
Cundinamarca	1	1.3	1.3	3.3	7.9	5.10%
Others	1.9	3.4	7.4	9.1	29.6	19.00%
Total	45.7	69.2	96.5	103.3	155.8	100%

Source: Meisel et al. (2014)

2015). A higher prevalence of family farming in the west contrasted with the estates in the east, where labour relations were more hierarchical. According to this thesis, the higher share of small farming plots in the west were more productive, and this led to the development of more inclusive institutions, which allowed peasants to take a greater share of the coffee production.

As important as the farm sizes were in the surge of coffee exports on a large scale in the west, they could not explain in full the reason for western Colombia's success. In northern Santander (East), the prevalence of small size or family farms in coffee production was significant (Bejarano, 2015), even more so than the successful regions in the west, such as Tolima. The transportation infrastructure was certainly a key factor behind the geographical divergence between east and west as steam technology was not evenly absorbed around the country.

3.3 The Dance of the Millions

The high economic growth rates reached in the 1920s were fuelled by the massive influx of capital that Colombia received during that period, which allowed the construction of necessary transport infrastructures, which in turn enabled the expansion of coffee exports. From late 1928 onwards, however, the economy began to slowdown. This was noted by the government's opposition leaders in the Liberal party (Junguito, 2018). The government's critics put forward the notion that the decline in the growth rate was due to the excessive increase in external

Table 3.6 Drivers of economic growth, 1905–1996

Period	*GDP growth*	*Contribution of capital*	*Contribution of labour force*	*TFP*
1905–1922	5.36	0.49	1.14	3.74
1923–1933	5.16	1.1	1.14	2.91
1905–1996	4.74	1.4	1.43	1,90

Source: Estimated based on Urrutia et al. (2002)
Note: The numbers for the periods 1905–1996 were taken from Urrutia et al. (2002, p. 15). Indicators for the periods 1905 and 1922 and 1925–1933 were estimated using data from the same authors, as well as coefficient the elasticity of capital on the GDP, $\alpha = 0.42$, what they estimated for the twentieth century. 1925 is the slicing year of two series of capital growth (1905–1924 and 1925–1996), which is why it was assumed that the capital growth for that year was an average between 1924 and 1926

debt, the so-called ***prosperidad al debe*** (prosperity by debt). These observers pointed out the government misspending of resources in the 1920s in costly public works of low benefit for the country's economy, in contemporaries known as la ***danza de los millones*** (the dance of the millions).

A relevant question to put against Colombian economic history is *how important was the government's role, particularly its significant investment in public infrastructure, for Colombia's take-off?* Based on the estimations of Urrutia et al. (2002), Table 3.6 shows the real GDP growth rate broken down into by its drivers; capital, labour, and technology, according the Slow-Swan model. Table 3.6 presents the Total Factor Productivity (TFP), which could be interpreted as an indicator of productivity, or the contribution of technology to economic growth. This indicator maintains that the high economic growth rate achieved by Colombia between 1905 and 1922 was mainly due to the TFP or productivity growth.

Productivity remained as the main driver for growth between 1923 and 1933, but at a slower pace as it declined to 2.91% from 3.74% observed in the period 1905–1922. In both cases, however, the level of productivity growth is higher than average for most of the twentieth century (1.9). The high growth rate of productivity in the 1910s and 1920s reinforces the thesis that it was the incorporation of steam into Colombia's economy was the main factor behind Colombia's economic take-off. The absorption of this general purpose technology, through the railways and steam navigation, made the rise of an export-led growth economy possible in the west of the country. The national government's heavy investment in transport infrastructure from 1923 onwards reinforced that trend, but its effects were much more moderate than in the period between 1905 and 1922, when the involvement of the regional government of Antioquia and the private sector (in steam navigation on the Magdalena River) was more intense.

A relevant question about Colombia's economic growth is; *why did productivity growth slowdown from 1923 onwards despite the massive increase in capital investment?* Indeed, the contribution of capital to economic growth more than doubled during the period of 1923–1933 compared to the level observed in 1905–1922. Considering Colombia's low starting point in the early twentieth century and its distance from the technological leaders, an evident question to pose is *how efficient was the government in allocating resources for transport infrastructure?*

Table 3.7 shows the revenue/expenditure ratio for the main Colombian railways. The most profitable railways in the early 1920s were the Antioquia and North railway (track 2), which saw revenues that were on average more than double that of their respective expenditure. The Girardot railway, which served the Bogota area, was also highly profitable as it was integrated with trade on the Magdalena River. The actual fact is that the government did not focus their investment on the most profitable railways, but concentrated its focus only on the Pacific railway, which did not perform particularly well.

The government's decision with regard to investment had a deep impact on the rate of return for railway investments, as the resources did not go there, they could be more profitable. Figure 3.7 presents the

Table 3.7 Revenue/expenditure ratio for the main Colombia railways, 1920–1925

Year	*Railways that served ports on Magdalena River in the 1910s*		*Railways serving the Buenaventura Port in 1923*		*Railways in the East of Colombia*		*All railways (included these no presented in the table) (%)*
	Antioquia (%)	*Girardot (%)*	*Caldas (%)*	*Pacífico (%)*	*Norte 2 (%)*	*Cúcuta (%)*	
1920	200	128.20	103.10	98.00	N/A	N/A	159
1921	238	151.50	149.30	109.90	227.30	128	145
1922	204	175.40	166.70	133.30	208.30	127	141
1923	238	172.40	166.70	144.90	217.40	179	154
1924	238	217.40	196.10	178.60	256.40	182	152
1925	222	227.30	140.80	175.40	156.30	164	147

Source: Meisel et al. (2014)

accumulated rate of return index of the government's investment in Colombia's main railways. The disparities in profitability between lines were huge, and the Pacific railway showed the poorest performance of all the railways presented in Fig. 3.7. As the Pacific railway harvested a substantial share of government investment, the index of accumulated return for Colombia was enormously lower than one where the Antioquia and the Cucuta railways would have contributed a higher share.

Considering the over-investment in the Pacific railway, opposition leaders were probably right when they accused the government of misspending its vast financial resources. The dance of the millions conjecture was proven correct, and the low profitability massively invested in railways is a key element of why the TFP was lower between 1923 and 1933 compared to the period 1905–1922. In the latter, the more profitable railways, especially the Antioquia railway, saw a concentration of the economy's investment, while during the former a significant share of the capital went to a less profitable investment.

A potential explanation of why the Pacific railway experienced such low profitability could be its poor integration to the rest of the regions, beyond

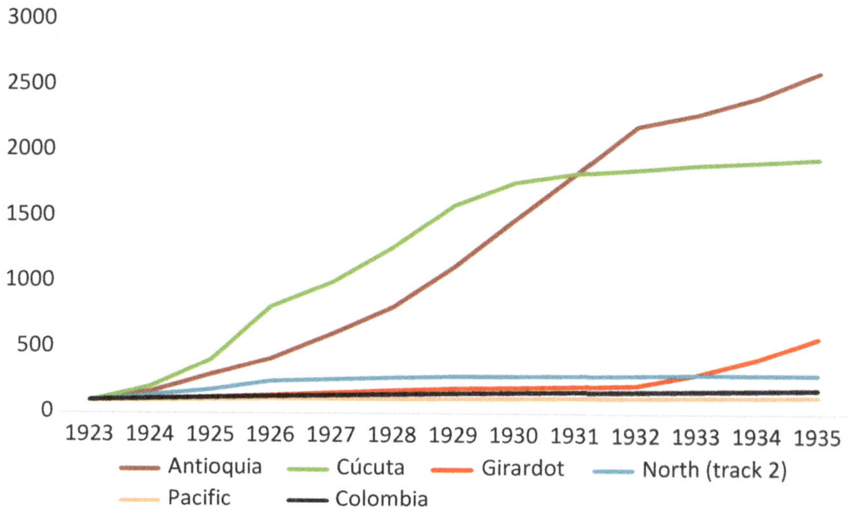

Fig. 3.7 Accumulated rate of return index of the government's investment in railways, 1923–1935 (1923 = 100) (Source: Estimated based on Meisel et al., 2014)

Caldas, which made it relatively isolated from most of the country. This was fundamental with the Antioquia railway, which was integrated to the rest of the country by the Magdalena River. The government's investments could have improved the transport infrastructure in a way that maximised network externality, for instance, linking and extending the lines already in operation, such as the Antioquia, La Dorada, or Girardot lines. A good alternative was envisioned by an American diplomat, as was discussed in Chap. 2, who favoured a line between Antioquia and Cartagena, replacing slow steam navigation on the Magdalena River.

Colombia could have better utilised the vast resources from the Panama indemnity, by building a modern transportation network, and maximising the potential of steam as a driver for economic growth. Economic performance, however, for the period of 1905–1929, was still good enough to allow Colombia's economic take-off, and left behind the secular stagnation of the late nineteenth century.

3.4 The Take-off and Improvements in the Standards of Living

Colombia's economic take-off not only meant a rise in GDP per capita, but also a substantial improvement in the standards of living. The economic growth of the early twentieth century certainly spread to a significant share of the population, which enjoyed an enhancement in quality of life, never seen before in Colombian history. Table 3.8 presents the poverty rate for Argentina, Chile, Colombia, and Mexico between 1913 and 1938, with estimates based on the estimations of Prados de la Escosura (2007). The poverty rate reduced to 70% in 1929, from 90% in 1913. As could be expected, before the economic take-off, almost all of Colombia's population was living below the poverty line, and it was the economic take-off

Table 3.8 Poverty head count, 1913–1938

Country	*1913*	*1929*	*1938*
Argentina	58	41	45
Chile	65	47	42
Colombia	90	70	65
Mexico	43	31	36

Source: Prados de la Escosura (2007)

that allowed a significant share of the population to move beyond the subsistence welfare level which characterised the pre-modern economies.

Poverty reduction in the early twentieth century is in line with the findings of Meisel and Vega (2007), for Colombia on average height, which has been widely used as a measurement of welfare by the economic history scholarship (Komlos, 1994). This indicator has an advantage over other welfare indicators, such as real wage or poverty, that is not affected by changes in consumption, quality of goods, or the incorporation of new products. Table 3.9 shows the average Colombian height between 1905 and 1944, revealing a substantial increase in the mean stature. Meisel and Vega (2007) concluded that one of the main factors behind such a notable increase in Colombian height was the improvements in nutrition, which was favoured by the developments in transportation. This development allowed an important decline in the real price of key agricultural products for the population's diet. Pachon and Ramirez (2006) found a negative relationship between transport infrastructure and important commodities for the population's diet, such as corn, potato, and rice in the twentieth century.

Improvements in nutrition also contributed to an increase in life expectancy, which rose to 34.2 years from only 29 in 1900. These levels certainly look terrible when compared to contemporary standards, but again, this was the norm in pre-modern economies. Colombia's take-off initiated an upward trend in life expectancy, which was reinforced by enhancements in sanitary conditions and medicine throughout the entire twentieth century, leading to an average life expectancy of 74.4 years by 2016.

Table 3.9 Average Colombian height by birth cohort, 1905–1944

Birth year	*Average height of men*	*Change in average height of men*	*Average height of women*	*Change in average height of women*
1905–1909	162.05		150.02	
1910–1914	163.48	1.43	150.78	0.76
1915–1919	163.61	0.13	151.49	0.71
1920–1924	164.16	0.55	152.38	0.89
1925–1929	164.7	0.54	153.06	0.68
1930–1934	165.17	0.47	153.48	0.42
1935–1939	165.76	0.59	154.21	0.73
1940–1944	166.26	0.50	154.69	0.48

Source: Meisel and Vega (2007)

Table 3.10 Historical Human Development Index,[a] 1900–1930

Year	*Argentina*	*Chile*	*Colombia*	*Mexico*
1900	0.46	0.35	0.26	0.22
1910	0.53	0.40	0.29	0.27
1920	0.58	0.43	0.33	0.33
1930	0.64	0.50	0.39	0.32

Source: Estimated based on MOxLAD (n.d.) for life expectancy and literacy, and Maddison Project Database for GDP per capita

[a]This index uses the GDP per capita in 2011 US dollars

Similarly, literacy rates increased from 34% to 52% in the first three decades of the twentieth century. Despite the fact that the huge leap in mass schooling only occurred in Colombia after 1950 (Ramirez & Tellez, 2007), political stability after the One Thousand Days War allowed the government to allocate more resources to primary schooling.

The improvements in real GDP per capita, education, and life expectancy indicates an increase in the Human Development Index (HDI), a composite indicator used by the United Nations to measure a country's level of development based on these three elements. The HDI uses school enrolment as a measurement of education, which is difficult to estimate for any period prior to 1960, due to the lack of data. This constraint has been overtaken by economic history scholars, who use the Historical Human Development Index (HHDI) (Astorga, Berges, & Fitzgerald, 2005; Prados de la Escosura, 2015). This index uses the rate of literacy instead of school enrolment as the indicator for education. The results for HHDI between 1900 and 1930 are presented in Table 3.10. Again, this indicator shows evidence of a substantial increase in the population's welfare during the Colombian take-off period. In 1930, Colombia's HHDI was higher than that of Mexico, but lower than that of the southern cone countries, which is in line with GDP per capita behaviour. Colombia saw significant welfare progress in the early twentieth century, and it was significant enough to converge with Argentina and Chile.

A final point to consider in this chapter is *how equally were the benefits of the Colombian take-off distributed?* Figure 3.8 shows the Gini coefficient for the four countries studied in this book between 1913 and 1950. In 1929, Colombia's Gini coefficient reached its lowest point with a level of 40.2, considerably inferior to the 46.8 observed in 1913. The actual fact is that by 1929, Colombia achieved its most egalitarian income distribution

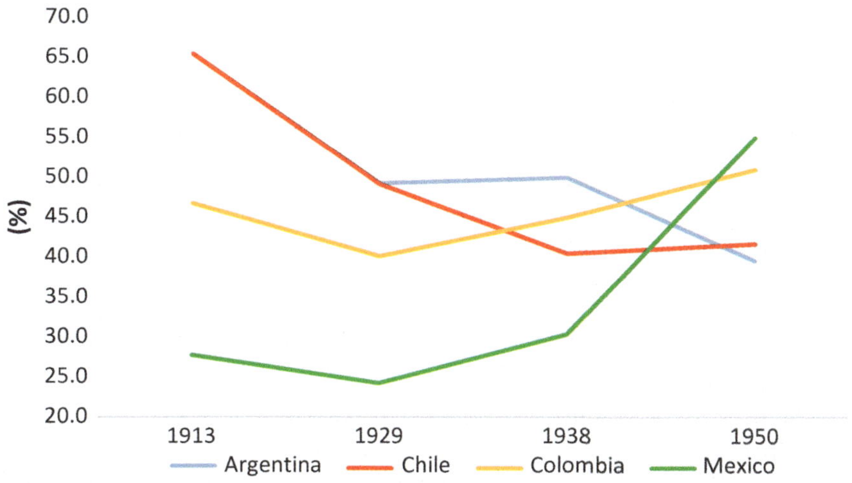

Fig. 3.8 Gini Index, 1913–1950 (Source: Prados de la Escosura, 2007)

for the last two centuries, pointing out that the benefits of its economic prosperity were widely dispersed among the population.

Colombia's economic take-off made the country richer, healthier, and in summary enhanced the population's standards of living, and an improvement in income distribution was observed. Colombia remained being a developing country, but despite all inconveniences and the long way ahead to development, Colombia in 1929 seemed like a distant relative of the impoverished, fragmented, and unstable country of 1900. The long-lasting stagnation of the late nineteen century finally came to an end, and the door of economic prosperity was finally opened.

References

Astorga, P., Berges, A., & Fitzgerald, V. (2005). The Standard of Living in Latin America during the Twentieth Century. *The Economic History Review, 58*, 765–796.

Bejarano, J. (2015). El despegue Cafetero (1900–1928). In J. Ocampo (Ed.), *Historia Económica de Colombia*. Bogota: Fondo de Cultura Económica.

Contraloría General de la República. (n.d.). *Anuario General de Estadística*. Several Years.

Global Financial Data Finaeon. (n.d.). *Global Financial Data Database and Indices*. Retrieved from http://www.globalfinancialdata.com/

Junguito, R. (2018). *Cien Episodios de la Historia Económica de Colombia*. Bogota: Ariel.

Komlos, J. (1994). *Stature, Living Standards, and Economic Development, Essays in Antropometric History*. Chicago: University of Chicago Press.

Maddison Project Database, Version 2018. Bolt, Jutta, Robert Inklaar, Herman de Jong and Jan Luiten van Zanden. (2018). *Rebasing 'Maddison': New Income Comparisons and the Shape of Long-Run Economic Development*. Retrieved from https://www.rug.nl/ggdc/historicaldevelopment/maddison/releases/maddison-project-database-2018

McGreevy, W. (1971). *An Economic History of Colombia, 1845–1930* (Latin America Studies Series). London: Cambridge University Press.

Meisel, A., Ramirez, M., & Jaramillo, J. (2014). Muy tarde pero rentables: Los ferrocarriles en Colombia durante el periodo 1920–1950. *Cuadernos de Historia Económica y Empresarial*, No. 34.

Meisel, A., & Vega, M. (2007). *La calidad de vida biológica en Colombia: antropometría histórica 1870–2003*. Banco de la Republica de Colombia.

Melo, J. (2015). Las Vicisitudes del Modelo Liberal (1850–1899). In J. Ocampo (Ed.), *Historia Económica De Colombia* (4th ed.). Bogota: Fondo de Cultura Economica/Fedesarrollo.

MOxLAD. (n.d.). Montevideo-Oxford Latin America Economic History Database. Retrieved from http://moxlad.cienciassociales.edu.uy/

Ocampo, J. (2015). *Historia Económica de Colombia*. Bogota: Fondo de Cultura Económica.

Pachon, A., & Ramirez, M. T. (2006). *La Infraestructura de Transporte en Colombia Durante el Siglo XX*. Bogota: Fondo de Cultura Económica/Banco de la República.

Prados de la Escosura, L. (2007). Inequality and Poverty in Latin America: A Long-Run Exploration. In T. Hatton, K. O'Rourke, & A. Taylor (Eds.), *The New Comparative Economic History. Essays in Honor of Jeffrey G. Williamson*. Cambridge, MA: The MIT Press.

Prados de la Escosura, L. (2015). World Human Development: 1870–2007. *Review of Income and Wealth, 61*, 220–247.

Ramirez, M., & Tellez, J. (2007). *La educación primaria y secundaria en Colombia en el siglo XX*. In M. Urrutia & J. Robinson (Eds.), *Economía colombiana del siglo XX: un análisis cuantitativo*. Bogota: Fondo de Cultura Económica.

Urrutia, M., Pontón, A., & Posada, C. (2002). *El Crecimiento Económico Colombiano En El Siglo XX*. Bogotá: Fondo de Cultura Eonómica.

CHAPTER 4

The Liberal Republic, 1930–1945: Overcoming the Great Depression, the Rise of Interventionism, and Economic Slowdown

Abstract Between 1930 and 1945, Colombia initiated a process of industrialisation by import substitution, but it could not be completed as the industry did not expand enough into exporting. On the other hand, Mexico saw an accelerated industrialisation based on the textile industry, which developed by substituting imports in the 1930s, and was propelled by its exports to the United States during the Second World War.

Why did Colombia not follow the same path as Mexico? The answer lies in that, unlike the latter, Colombia was not able to absorb mass production technology on a larger scale. In this period, Colombia implemented economic reforms, which meant a mobilisation of resources towards one favoured sector: coffee. This fact led to a considerable underinvestment in the manufacturing industry and services.

Keywords Import-substitution industrialisation • Economic slowdown • Protectionism • Mass production • Textiles • External debt • Mexico

The presidential election of 1930 was a watershed in Colombia's economic history, as the Liberal party returned to power after more than 50 years acting as the opposition. The victory of the liberal candidate, President Enrique Olaya Herrera, ended a long conservative hegemony in

I. Luzardo-Luna, *Colombia's Slow Economic Growth*,
Palgrave Studies in Economic History,
https://doi.org/10.1007/978-3-030-25755-2_4

Colombia, which included its radical form with *La Regeneración* (1880–1904), as well as a moderate version of it (1904–1930). The implications of such an important change went beyond politics, and had long-lasting consequences on the Colombian economy.

The period between 1930 and 1945 is known in Colombian historiography as the Liberal Republic, because such a party governed uninterrupted for all these years. The new regime ruled sometimes with moderation, looking for consensus, as in the periods 1930–1934 and 1938–1942, and at other times in a more radical and confrontational way, as was the case for the periods of 1934–1938 and 1942–1945. In any case, the entire period entailed a transition towards an economy with increased government interventionism.

The government's interventionism in Colombia in the 1930s and 1940s has some features in common with the rest of Latin America, but it also has some peculiarities. In general terms, the government followed an orthodox approach with regard to fiscal and monetary policy, and focused its role on the control of the banking system and the external sector. The trauma created by hyperinflation throughout the regeneration era convinced the Colombian elite of how important it was to preserve price stability, which is why the government opted for prudence in such matters (Ocampo, 2015). The government's interventionism, however, cannot be underestimated as it profoundly shaped Colombia's relationship with the rest of the world, and affected the evolution of its financial sector.

Figure 4.1 shows real GDP per capital in logarithms for Argentina, Chile, Colombia, and Mexico. Considering the pattern of economic growth, the Liberal Republic could be split into three different periods: a mild Great Depression of 1929, sustained but slow growth, between 1932 and 1939, and prolonged recession from the onset of the Second World War. Unlike the other three countries studied in this book, the Great Depression did not lead to deep economic decline, and already in 1932, the economy began to expand again. The situation was very different during the Second World War, when Colombia saw its longest economic recession of the twentieth century, from 1940 up to 1944. During those years, the effects of the economic reforms implemented throughout the Liberal Republic era were felt and the economy moved into a pattern of slow growth, very different from that observed in the 1920s, and in some way remained operating under such a framework for the rest of the century. On the whole, the entire period could be classed as one of economic

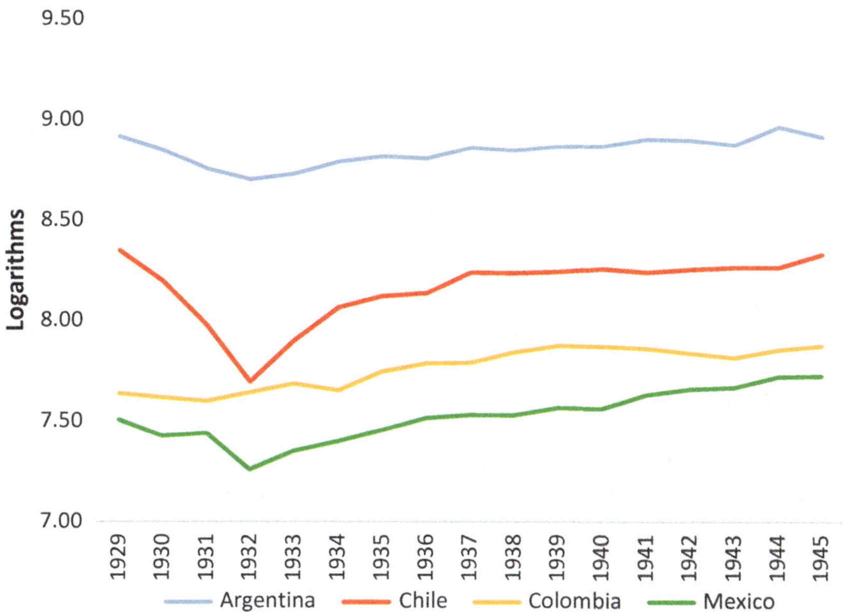

Fig. 4.1 Real GDP per capita at 2011 US$ prices (logs), 1929–1945 (Sources: Maddison Project Database, Version 2018. Bolt, Jutta, Robert Inklaar, Herman de Jong and Jan Luiten van Zanden (2018))

slowdown, but what was probably more important for the long-term growth trend, between 1930 and 1945, was that Colombia could not fully embrace the general purpose technology, which was the driver behind economic growth for most of the twentieth century: mass production.

4.1 Successful Management of the Great Depression

The Great Depression of 1929 affected the country in two main ways: the interruption of capital inflow and a huge decline in the international coffee price. From 1928, Colombia began to face problems continuing to contract fresh foreign debt as the fiscal situation of the country deteriorated. That situation was noted by the Department of Commerce of the United States, which issued a document in September 1928 warning their investors about the weak fiscal situation of the Colombian government

(Ocampo, 2015). As was discussed in Chap. 3, the vast expansion of transport infrastructure, especially in the second half of the 1920s, was to a large extent founded with external debt. The ratio of debt to GDP rose quickly from 2.6% in 1926 to 6.9% in 1928, while the fiscal deficit reached a level of 0.4% of the GDP, when the country had showed a fiscal surplus just two years previously.

Colombia's fiscal position was complex, but still far from collapse. The actual interruption of capital inflow came with the New York Stock Market crash in October 1929, which made it extremely difficult to find fresh funds in the foreign banking system, even with exemplary debtor behaviour. Likewise, in 1929, the international price of coffee went into strong decline (see Fig. 3.4), which meant a huge reduction in the country's access to hard currency and hence government revenue, as tariffs were still its main source of income.

The government's initial reaction to the crisis was very orthodox, and the new liberal government appointed experienced economists, who worked in the former conservative administration, for the management of the crisis. Colombia remained under the gold standard, and implemented enormous fiscal adjustment. With price stability as a top priority, the government's main policy action was an expenditure cut in the range of 60% to 70% during the period of 1928–1932 (Ocampo, 2015, p. 207). Also, in line with Colombia's commitment to the gold standard, the country witnessed substantial deflation of −21.7% in 1930, −13.4% in 1931, and −19.6% in 1932 (Junguito and Rincon, 2004). These measures were pro-cyclical, but cannot be underestimated as the government gained space and credibility for expansionary and counter-cyclical policies in the following years.

Certainly, one of the Colombian government's priorities was to maintain its access to foreign credit, probably aware of how costly it was, did not follow the rules of the capital markets in the late nineteenth century. Indeed, despite its precarious fiscal condition, the government continued serving the debt up to May 1932. From that month onwards up to early 1933, when the war against Peru complicated public finances even more, the government agreed with bondholders to only pay interest (Ocampo, 2015). During 1933 and 1934, the government continued honouring its debt, but rather than continuing the payments in dollars, the government issued treasury bills to be paid when the situation improved. It was only in 1935, under the new administration of President Alfonso López Pumarejo that the government ceased external debt payments completely.

The Colombian government moved to a more interventionist role in its economic management in late 1931, when the financial panic generated by Britain's abandonment of the gold standard on 19 September accelerated capital outflow from developing countries. The policy actions were concentrated into two areas: the external sector and the financial system.

The government's first step towards increased interventionism was the adoption of capital controls in September 1931. With the fear of inflation in mind, Colombia favoured capital controls as a policy response to the scarcity of hard currency, rather than exchange rate devaluation, as occurred in Mexico. In 1933, the United States abandoned the gold standard, which was followed by the Colombian government. At that point, the country implemented discriminatory devaluations, with a higher exchange rate for imports than the one paid for exports (Ocampo, 2015).

The rationale behind the devaluation with different exchange rates was to reduce imports, making them more costly, and support exports increasing their prices in domestic currency. As was anticipated, devaluation led to significant inflation (16.9%) in 1934 (Junguito and Rincon, 2004), but it was compensated for by strong deflation observed between 1930 and 1933. In that sense, the orthodox management of the monetary policy in the early phase of the crisis, allowed the government to adopt a counter-cyclical policy as devaluation, which is what allowed it to support economic recovery.

Alongside capital control, the government also intervened in the external sector with Law 62 of May 1931, which increased tariffs up to 15% and established that transportation firms must give priority to national food products and their services. It is worth noting that in February 1931, the congress approved Law 29, which established the *Consejo Administrativo de los Ferrocarriles Nacionales* (National Railways Administrative Agency) with the authority to regulate railway rates and itineraries. With such a new law, the government had strong discretionary powers, which is plausible to assume that they used to favour national companies in what was another step closer to increased protectionism.

The second element of the government's strategy was boosting credit. As the resources of international capital were not available, the government appealed to the Central Bank to obtain credit, and to also support large private agents, such as coffee exporters. Law 82 of June 1931 changed the Central Bank statutes incorporating one representative coffee exporter, one from industry, and one member of the Ministry of Finance in its board of directors. Such legal framework allowed the Central Bank to increase its loans to the government by advancing the monopoly salt revenues, publicly owned, when the economic situation became worse in late 1931 (Ocampo, 2015).

The credit boost strategy also included the foundation of three financial institutions in 1931: *La Caja Agraria* (Agricultural fund), *Banco Central Hipotecario-BCH* (Central Mortgage Bank), and *La Corporación Colombiana de Crédito* (Colombian Credit Corporation) (Ocampo, 2015, p. 208). The former had the main purpose of providing development credit to the agricultural sector, under conditions that were more favourable than commercial banks. On the other hand, the two other institutions were directed at supporting the portfolio restructuring of private banks. Besides supporting credit expansion, the government directly intervened in the banking system to reduce interest rates, extend loan payment deadlines, and allow debtors to pay half of their mortgage debts with government bonds (Ocampo, 2015, p. 208).

Table 4.1 presents the main macroeconomic variables between 1929 and 1934, which indicates that the drivers for Colombia's recovery were mainly from domestic demand rather than exports. In 1932, Colombia's real GDP was higher than the level observed in 1929, but exports continued declining, and only began to recover in 1934, most likely propelled by devaluations in 1933. As the driver for economic recovery was the internal market, it could be concluded that the policies implemented in 1931 directed at increasing credit, and providing financial relief to the private sector, worked well. Such policies focused on boosting credit, allowing Colombia to avoid a great depression, and it was able to move on from the crisis more swiftly than most of the other Latin America countries.

Table 4.1 Index for the main macroeconomic variables, 1929–1934 (1929 = 100)

Variable	*1929*	*1930*	*1931*	*1932*	*1933*	*1934*
Real GDP	100	99.1	97.5	104.0	109.8	116.7
Export	100	89.2	77.5	54.5	48.0	76.3
Imports	100	49.6	32.4	23.9	32.6	44.0
Inflation rate	100	78.3	67.8	54.5	53.8	62.9
Exchange rate	100	100.2	100.2	101.6	120.5	157.4

Source: Estimated based on Junguito and Rincon (2004)

4.2 The Rise of Government Interventionism and Economic Slowdown (1935–1939)

The end of the conservative hegemony in 1930 was largely influenced by the rise of new social groups, such as urban workers, whom the liberal party looked to attract to the field. Indeed, the government legalised trade unions and regulated the right to strike with Law 83 in 1931. The moderate government of President Enrique Olaya Herrera came to an end in August 1934, and was replaced with the more radical administration of President Alfonso López Pumarejo, and his programme known as *Revolución en Marcha* (Revolution in Progress), strongly influenced by the ideas of the *New Deal* (Bushnell, 1993, pp. 181–192). The latter made substantial social progress, such as the universal vote for men and land reforms to support peasants. The new administration, however, increased government control of the economy, especially in matters of foreign trade.

Late in 1937, the international coffee price declined again (see Fig. 3.4), which reduced the country's access to hard currency. With capital controls already in force from 1931, barriers to imports increased. In November 1937, the government split imports in two groups: essential, and non-essential, giving priority to the former. In April 1938, the government increased its protection over the textiles industry, temporarily banning almost all imports in that sector (Ocampo, 2015). Without doubt, Colombian protectionism moved to a new plateau, and what were emergency measures implemented to face the Great Depression, later became permanent features for most of the twentieth century.

Another area that complicated Colombia's relationship with the world economy was its external debt. At the beginning of López Pumarejo's administration, the bondholders contacted the new government through the Foreign Bondholders Protective Council-FBPC to explore an arrangement to resume debt payments, even applying pressure for a special tariff on Colombian coffee imported by the United States (Junguito, 2018). The government opted to reject the bondholder's appeal, and in 1935, completely stopped the interest payments that the country had served since early 1933 with treasury bills. It was only during the new more moderate administration of President Eduardo Santos (1938–1942) that Colombia embarked on serious negotiations with foreign investors. After several months of negotiations with the FBPC, in June 1941, the Colombian government launched an offer to the bondholders, which received endorsement by the Roosevelt administration, proposing an interest reduction to 3% from an original 6%, and 50% of the unpaid interest from 1935 (Avella, 2004). The FBPC rejected the offer terms, but left the decision in the bondholders' hands, the majority of which accepted the deal.

Probably the most well-known economic policy of López Pumarejo's administration was the tax reform introduced with Law 78, implemented on 23 December 1935. This reform, strengthened direct taxation in Colombia by increasing income tax at a progressive rate up to 17%, substantially higher than the maximum threshold of 8% that had been in force from 1928. In addition, the tax reform introduced two complementary taxes: equity, and profit surplus tax.

The tax reforms of 1935 substantially increased the government's revenue, which in turn increased its fiscal surplus. Despite the potential negative impact that such a tax increase could have had on investment, the actual fact is that the real GDP grew by 5.3% in 1936. Despite a significant decline to 1.6% in 1937, the economy expanded by over 6% in 1938 and 1939. Table 4.2 presents an index for the main macroeconomic variables for the period of 1934–1939. Analysing these variables, it becomes evident that the GDP was propelled by investments in fixed capital and not by exports (as it was during the export-led growth era of 1905–1929). Coffee exports remained essential as the main source of hard currency, but the driver for economic growth now mainly came from the internal market.

An interesting question is why did the tax reform of 1935 not lead to a slowdown in the investment of fixed capital between 1935 and 1939. A plausible explanation is that the new public resources were heavily channelled towards investment as what actually occurred with a vast amount of government investment in roads throughout these years. Table 4.3 shows the government's investment in railways and roads, as well as the

Table 4.2 Index for the main macroeconomic variables, 1934–1939 (1934 = 100)

Variable	*1934*	*1935*	*1936*	*1937*	*1938*	*1939*
Real GDP	100	102.4	107.8	109.6	116.7	123.8
Export	100	85.4	96.0	111.2	97.4	107.8
Imports	100	111.3	127.2	159.1	147.7	173.7
Inflation rate	100	100.0	100.0	100.0	100.0	100.0
Exchange rate	100	109.7	107.7	108.7	109.9	107.7
Gross fixed capital formation	100	114.3	126.0	146.0	149.5	170.7

Source: Estimated based on Junguito and Rincon (2004)

extension of these means of transportation. At its height (1927–1928), Colombia's investment in transportation accounted for more than 7% of its overall GDP, although it was focused on railways. With the Great Depression and its aftermath, the massive investment in transportation came to an end. Although the government continued to invest in transportation infrastructure, this time it focused on roads (see Fig. 4.2), which demanded lower mobilisation of resources. The increase in the government's revenues, obtained from the 1935 tax reforms, increased the government's expenditure capacity, which is why from this year onwards there was an acceleration in road construction. Between 1935 and 1939, Colombian roads expanded by 4854 kilometres, the fastest pace hitherto in actual terms.

Roads had a similar effect to railways in the early twentieth century, in that they spread the use of steam into Colombia's production capacity. In

Table 4.3 Investment and extension of railways and roads, 1925–1945

Year	*Investment (in millions of 1950 COP$)*	*Investments (% of GDP)*	*Kilometres of railways*	*Kilometres of roads*
1925	98.7	4.55	1826	3729
1926	154	6.45	2012	4053
1927	163	7.26	2216	4411
1928	191.9	7.66	2405	4809
1929	140.6	5.33	2587	5251
1930	91.1	3.44	2549	5743
1931	73.3	3.02	2832	6537
1932	42	1.55	2819	7139
1933	55.2	1.85	2892	7799
1934	42.3	1.13	3056	8524
1935	53.1	1.30	3077	8928
1936	64.9	1.57	3035	9683
1937	75.2	1.96	3060	11,595
1938	80.9	1.98	3139	13,000
1939	108.8	2.53	3093	13,782
1940	121.9	2.65	3096	14,644
1941	96.3	1.55	3137	15,586
1942	92	2.00	3290	16,573
1943	104.3	2.21	3369	16,835
1944	95.8	1.99	3407	17,964
1945	90.4	1.67	3430	18,470

Source: Pachon and Ramirez (2006)

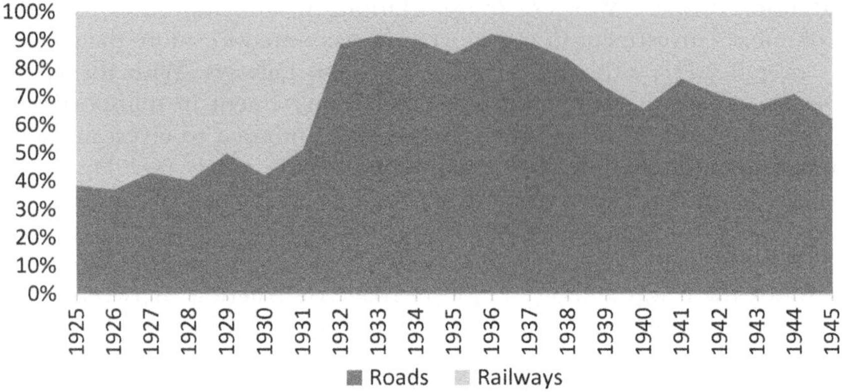

Fig. 4.2 Investment and extension of railways and roads, 1925–1945 (Source: Pachon & Ramirez, 2006)

fact, roads in the 1930s made something that was not possible to achieve with the railways in the 1920s—they conveyed steam technology to the east of Colombia. Table 4.4 presents the kilometres of roads by department for the years 1924 and 1945. In the middle of the 1920s, the few roads that Colombia had were mainly concentrated in Cundinamarca (Bogota's department), and the east in general. After the strong expansion during the Liberal Republic era, kilometres of roads grew more evenly between the east and west. The north, however, saw a more moderate increase.

Despite the improvements in transport infrastructure, the economic growth between 1935 and 1939 saw a slowdown, probably structural, relative to the levels observed between 1925 and 1929. While in the latter period, the real GDP per capita expanded by 7.0%, in the former, it expanded by only 4.4%. The general purpose technology that enabled such economic growth was steam in both cases, but it looks as though its impact was higher during the railway era than during the road era. This latter period however, spread the use of steam technology to the east of the country, which propelled economic growth in that region and reduced regional inequality.

One of the reasons why the accomplishment of roads was more moderate than railways was naturally because the magnitude of investment was much lower (see Table 4.3). The Colombian government paid a price in economic growth terms for debt moratorium between 1935–1941 due to

Table 4.4 Kilometres of roads by departments, 1924–1945

Region	*Kilometres of roads in 1924*	*Kilometres of roads per 1000 inhabitants 1924*[a]	*Kilometres of roads in 1945*	*Kilometres of roads per 1000 inhabitants 1945*[b]	*Kilometres of roads per kilometres of territory 1945*
East					
Cundinamarca	1683	1.59	2831	2.41	0.13
Boyaca	367	0.39	1408	1.91	0.02
Santander	302	0.51	1631	2.65	0.04
Norte de Santander	80	0.24	938	2.71	0.04
Total East	2432	0.83	6808	2.37	0.04
West					
Antioquia	234	0.23	2008	1.69	0.03
Caldas	0	–	1193	1.55	0.09
Cauca	120	0.38	851	2.39	0.03
Huila	30	0.14	1000	4.62	0.04
Nariño	240	0.58	1397	3.00	0.04
Tolima	49	0.11	766	1.40	0.03
Valle	298	0.59	1462	2.38	0.07
Total West	971	0.28	8677	2.09	0.04
North					
Atlantico	0	–	393	1.46	0.13
Bolivar	30	0.05	882	1.15	0.01
Magdalena	4	0.01	1127	3.29	0.02
Total North	34	0.03	2402	1.75	0.02
Intendencias	0	–	613	3.49	0.00
Grand total	3437	0.44	18,500	2.16	0.03

Source: Estimated based on Pachon and Ramirez (2006)

Note: 1928 extension and population based on 1929 anuario estadistico. It does not include comisarias: Arauca, Caqueta, Guajira, Putumayo, Vaupes, Vichada

[a]Based on 1928 census

[b]Based on 1938 census

the country not being able to secure fresh loans from foreign markets, of which the capital could not be completely replaced by direct government revenues. President Santos Montejo (1938–1942) was aware of that, and mentioned the issue in his inauguration speech, and actively looked for an agreement with the American and British bondholders. In a meeting that took place early in his administration with a British delegation in Bogota, President Santos Montejo mentioned that he has in mind '***the possibility of a combined agreement with the grant of new loans from England to develop*** *new industries in Colombia*' (Avella, 2004). Unfortunately, when the negotiations concluded in 1940, and Colombia resumed its payments in 1941, the funding from London and New York was not availed as the world was already in the midst of the Second World War.

4.3 The Second World War: A Long-Lasting Stagnation

In 1940, the economic growth rate declined to 2.2%, from the 6.1% reached in 1939 (see Table 4.5). The main reason behind the economic slowdown was the decline in exports which were heavily impacted by a new reduction in international coffee prices. The government reacted to this situation, which meant bringing with it a scarcity of hard currency, an increase in imports control, and, in April 1940, the establishment of a surcharge on the exchange rate for imports (Ocampo, 2015, p. 212).

Besides the poor performance of exports, the growth rate in the 1940s was also impacted by a decline in investment. As can be observed in Table 4.5, the gross fixed capital formation declined significantly between 1940 and 1942, and was the main driver behind economic stagnation in that period. In 1939, the government strengthened its long-term developing credit policy through the foundation of three new institutions: *Instituto de Crédito Territorial* (Regional Credit Institute), *Fondo Nacional de Ganadería* (National Livestock Fund), and *Instituto de Fomento Industria* (Industrial Development Institute). Considering the path of gross fixed capital formation, however, such an increase in credit did not have the same results as that of the 1931, when it worked effectively as a counter-cyclical policy.

Table 4.5 Growth rates for main macroeconomic variables, 1939–1945

Variable	*1939 (%)*	*1940 (%)*	*1941 (%)*	*1942 (%)*	*1943 (%)*	*1944 (%)*	*1945 (%)*
GDP	6.10	2.20	1.70	0.20	0.40	6.80	4.70
Exports	10.70	−5.20	4.80	9.10	14.30	4.00	8.00
Imports	17.60	−19.20	14.60	−38.20	40.10	19.20	60.50
Gross fixed capital formation	14.20	−4.00	−4.30	−12.10	6.10	8.90	24.50
Inflation rate	4.40	−3.10	−1.40	8.70	15.90	20.30	11.30
Monetary base	7.20	2.90	8.90	21.30	28.90	38.20	14.60

Source: Junguito and Rincon (2004)

The decline in imports generated scarcity of some essential inputs (Ocampo, 2015), which alongside an acceleration in the monetary base, conduced a rise in inflation. Likewise, the reduction in imports led to a deterioration in the government's revenue coming from tariffs, which remained an important source of resources for the public administration. The accumulated efforts of the liberal policies from 1931 to reduce imports led Colombia to the unfortunate situation of stagnation combined with inflation in 1942.

Also in 1942, there was a presidential election, and President Alfonso López Pumarejo returned to government for a second term (1942–1945). In his second administration, President López would increase government interventionism even more by establishing a surcharge of 35% on revenue tax, and issued *Bonos de Defensa Económica Nacional* (National Economy Defense Bonds), which remained in force up to 1945. The latter had to be purchased compulsorily by the revenue tax payer with a sum equivalent to 50% of their tax payments in 1942 and 1943. Likewise, the financial institutions should have had to purchase such bonds with a sum equal to 20% of their deposits, the insurance and industrial firms with 10% of their reserves, and the National Coffee Fund with 20% of its revenues (Ocampo, 2015, p. 213).

In 1943, the government relieved import controls and removed the surcharges that had been introduced in 1940, which resulted in a significant increase in imports (40.1%). At the same time, the government increased the commercial banks' reserve ratio, and ordered for high income taxpayers and big companies to invest 20% of their profits in Central Bank bills. With these measures, Colombia moved one step forward towards interventionism in the banking system, reinforcing the Central Bank as a development bank and as the government's regular lender.

The result of government policies against the external sector and financial system, plus low international coffee prices, basically led to the stagnation of aggregate GDP growth between 1940 and 1943. Due to population growth being high during such years, Colombia saw a decline in its real GDP per capita of –5.9%[1] over the three years. Even in 1945, the real GDP per capita was slightly lower than the one it reached in 1939. Such

[1] According to Maddison Project Database, version (2018). Bolt, Jutta, Robert Inklaar, Herman de Jong and Jan Luiten van Zanden (2018), 'Rebasing "Maddison": new income comparisons and the shape of long-run economic development'.

performance was the opposite of what occurred in Mexico (see Fig. 4.1), which in the same period saw an increase in its real GDP of 17.2%.

Why did Colombia not follow the same path as Mexico between 1940 and 1943? The answer probably lies in that unlike the former, the latter was able to absorb mass production technology on a large scale because of more rapid industrialisation. Such progress meant the consolidation of an industrial sector, which became and has remained as the core of Mexico's exports up to the twenty-first century. The cornerstone of that industrialisation was the textile industry, which developed by substituting imports in the 1930s, and was propelled by its exports to the United States during the Second World War (Cardenas, 2000).

As with most Latin American countries, Mexico was significantly affected by the Great Depression which interrupted its exports to the United States. The policy response was to strongly devalue the exchange rate. The long border with the United States, and the high degree of integration between the two economies made capital controls unfeasible, and this explained why the government did not opt for such a policy (Cardenas, 2000), as was the case for Colombia.

The devaluation of the exchange rate made imports more costly, which alongside a strengthening in the purchasing power led to strong import substitution of consumer goods, such as in the textile and processed food industries. The import-substitution industrialisation of Mexico in the 1930s, although supported by the state, was to a large extent a market-driven phenomenon (Cardenas, 2000). Between 1932 and 1940, real industrial production grew 118% (Cardenas, 2000, p. 180), which meant an average annual rate of over 10%.

Colombia's industrial growth in the 1930s was even higher than that of Mexico. Between 1931 and 1939, real industrial production increased at an annual average rate of 12.1% (Ocampo, 2015, p. 227). As for Mexico, Colombia's industry was essentially expanding through imports substitution in the 1930s, as can be observed in the case of the cotton textile industry presented in Table 4.6. In 1934, around 80% of the cotton textiles consumed in Colombia were imported, but in 1942, this share declined to only 5.7%. It was during the Second World War, however, that Colombia witnessed its greatest expansion as domestic production could supply the massive growth in consumption. Despite Colombia's textile industry starting to export in 1942, its focus remained on the internal market.

The onset of the Second World War was a watershed for the development of the industrial sector in Colombia and Mexico. For Colombia, the

Table 4.6 Imports, production, and exports of cotton textiles, 1934–1945 (thousands of metres)

Year	*Imports*	*Domestic production*	*Exports*	*Apparent consumption*	*Share of domestic demand supplied by imports (%)*
1934	83,357	20,274	–	103,631	80.4
1937	96,089	43,130	–	139,219	69.0
1939	69,710	69,644	–	139,354	50.0
1940	29,631	73,490	–	103,121	28.7
1942	6700	110,817	2343	115,174	5.7
1945	8596	141,453	9156	140,893	5.7

Source: Montenegro (1982, p. 154)

war meant a substantial slowdown (Kalmanovitz, 2017, p. 204), while for Mexico it was the driver to forging ahead in its expansion, as it began to export industrial products to the United States on a significant scale (Cardenas, 2000). Mexico was part of the American resource mobilisation for the Second World War, which was reinforced with a trade agreement in 1943. Such a trade relationship favoured Mexico's industrial sector, which by then accounted for almost 38% of total exports (Cardenas, 2000, p. 183).

The fundamental difference between the Colombian and Mexican textile industries, was that the latter moved to exportation during the Second World War. On the other hand, Colombia continued exporting mainly coffee, which between 1942 and 1945 accounted for more than 70% of Colombia's exports. Such a situation leads one to wonder why did not the Colombian industry sector, specifically the textile industry, move to export in the Second World War? The most probable answer lies in the fact that government interventionism in Colombia in some way meant a mobilisation of resources from the whole economy towards one favoured sector: coffee. That was the opposite of what occurred in Mexico, where President Lazaro Cardenas' policies against agriculture and the oil industry led to the mobilisation of resources from such sectors towards industry (Cardenas, 2000, p. 180).

This situation can be illustrated with a general equilibrium model, in which there are two sectors in the economy[2] (K_1, and K_2). In this model, without government intervention, the relative allocation of capital depends on the productivity of each sector, as is presented in Eq. 4.1:

[2] As the one used by Bergoeing et al. (2002).

$$\frac{K_1}{K_2} = \left(\frac{A_1}{A_2} \right)^{\frac{1}{1-\alpha}} \tag{4.1}$$

$$\frac{K_1}{K_2} = \left(\frac{A_1}{A_2} \right)^{\frac{1}{(1-\alpha)}} \left(\frac{1+\tau_2}{1-\tau_1} \right)^{\frac{1}{1-\alpha}} \tag{4.2}$$

As Bergoeing, Kehoe, Kehoe, and Soto (2002) show, the government could intervene in the economy by subsidising sector 1 with τ_1. In order to fund the subsidy, the government needs resources which it obtains by taxing sector 2 with τ_2. In such a situation, the relative allocation of capital will be given by Eq. 4.2.

In this second case, the investment decision does not depend anymore only on the productivity in each sector, but also on the size of the government subsidies. In such a situation, there will be an overinvestment in the favoured sector, and an underinvestment in the other sector.

That was probably what was going on in Colombia in the late 1930s. The Colombian government heavily supported the coffee sector, which meant a transfer of resources to such a sector from the rest of the economy. This fact led to a considerable underinvestment in the other sectors, particularly the manufacturing industry, which due to the discovery of mass production technology and a low starting point, had huge potential for productivity gains.

In 1927, the *Federación Nacional de Cafeteros-Fedecafe* (National Federation of Coffee Growers) was founded, which was the trade association for coffee cultivators. Such an organisation became so influential in Colombian institutions, especially on government credit policy, that it even designated a member to the Central Bank board during the 1931 reforms. In the same year, the coffee producers were supported by financial relief implemented in these years for the agricultural sector, plus a special exchange rate. The power of the Fedecafe however, saw its main increase in 1940 when Colombia signed the Inter-American Coffee Agreement, where the United States established import quotas to exporter countries. In order to fulfil the agreement, the government and Fedecafe established the *Fondo Nacional del Café* (National Coffee Fund), which was in charge of buying and storing the coffee produced, which could exceed Colombia's quota.

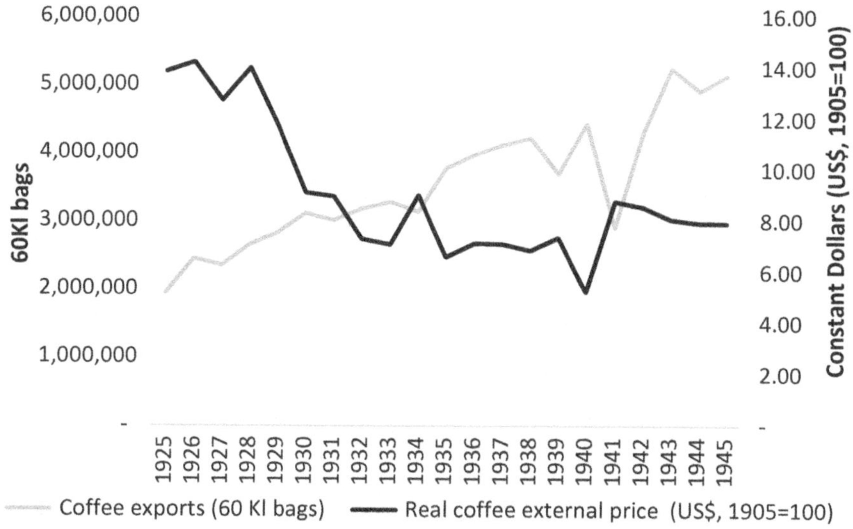

Fig. 4.3 Coffee volume exports (60 kg) and real coffee external price, 1925–1945 (Source: Urrutia, Pontón, & Posada, 2002)

The operation of the Coffee Fund was very profitable, and in 1943, that institution accumulated capital of COP$ 88 million, which was more than half the government's revenue at that time (Ocampo, 2015, p. 217). The privileged access to development credit probably explains the mobilisation of resources towards this sector. Despite low international coffee prices, and higher taxes, coffee exports steadily increased in the 1930s and early 1940s (in volume terms), except in 1941 (see Fig. 4.3). In that sense, it is plausible to assume that the reason why investment continued mainly being directed towards coffee production, rather than to industries such as textiles, was the significant government support.

The textile industry showed outstanding performance during the Second World War, as can be seen in Table 4.6, although unlike Mexico it could not move to exportation. A key reason why the Colombian textile industry remained focused mainly on its domestic market is that production prices were not competitive in the international market. Table 4.7 presents the index of relative price for the import of cotton textiles with regard to domestic production prices. It can be noted that, despite Colombian produced textiles being competitive in 1937, this advantage dissipated by 1941, when imported cotton textiles became more affordable. Between 1941 and 1943, Colombian cotton textiles reversed this

Table 4.7 Index of relative prices for cotton textile, 1926–1943

Year	*Ratio of import price to production price*	*Ratio of production price to a metre of imported cotton price*	*Ratio of production price to wages*	*Ratio of production price to whole food price index*
1926	100	100	100	100
1929	101.4	99.1	88.1	104.7
1931	87.9	146.5	108.0	147.9
1937	120.3	86.4	99.4	140.3
1939	112.0	107.4	86.6	114.8
1941	88.3	148.5	122.4	172.0
1943	109.9	143.7	104.2	152.3

Source: Montenegro (1982)

Table 4.8 Textile, transport, and total machinery real value imports, 1934–1945 (millions of constant USD, 1947–1949 = 100)

Year	*Textile machinery imports*	*Transport machinery imports*	*Total machinery imports*
1934	2235	6971	14,728
1935	1213	6416	16,125
1936	658	9681	20,682
1937	2944	11,028	29,011
1938	2520	11,376	29,800
1939	2529	15,172	34,980
1940	2568	10,382	29,190
1941	2849	13,113	29,084
1942	1500	3046	10,118
1943	2343	2923	13,699
1944	1477	6667	18,246
1945	3356	12,265	41,412

Source: Montenegro (1982)

trend and became competitive but probably not enough so as to lead towards a movement of large scale export.

Table 4.7 also shows that the reasons behind the worsening in Colombian cotton textile international competitiveness were substantial increments in imported cotton (an essential input) and labour costs. A natural economic response to higher labour costs is the substitution of workers with capital. Such transition towards more capital-intensive production, however, required machinery imports which government protectionism made difficult. Table 4.8 shows that real value imports of textile machinery increased in 1937, but stalled in the years going forward. In addition, the exchange rate differential policy, which favoured coffee exporters but taxed importers, worked against an increase in the use of technology in the textile industry. The lack of access to international capital markets did not favour textile machinery imports either.

With the lack of competitiveness in international markets in the Second World War, the only way in which the Colombian textile industry could grow was by import substitution rather than exporting. In that sense, the factories in inland regions with the largest internal market, and where imports were more costly to transport, grew faster than those located on the north coast. The latter had a higher potential for exporting but small local markets. In the late 1920s, Barranquilla had the largest textile firm in Colombia, the *Fabrica de Tejidos Obregon*, with almost double the quantity of looms than the second and third placed firms located in Medellin (Montenegro, 1982). By the end of the Second World War, the situation was completely different, and Medellin as a city, and Antioquia as a region, were consolidated as Colombia's industrial powerhouse.

The rise of Antioquia as Colombia's industrial centre is not surprising considering the vast resources that this region received from the coffee business. As was noted by Ocampo (2015), the lack of a proper financial market made especially relevant the family ties as a way of funding industrial ventures with the resources coming from agriculture or trade. Coffee being the main economic sector in the country, these factories located in the coffee cultivating regions probably had a higher charge in obtaining funding than those located in the north or the east.

In general terms, the Liberal Republic was very successful in coping the Great Depression of 1929, which the country managed to overcome relatively quickly. Liberal rule, however, moved Colombia towards protectionism against foreign trade, as well as high interventionism in the financial sector, which prevented the country from utilising mass production technology, and to increase its economic growth. Colombia could have initiated the process of industrialisation by import substitution, but it could not be completed as the industry did not expand enough into exporting. This trend toward a more interventionist role of government was, however, just starting. Colombia would increase its protectionism even more on trade, and its intervention in the financial sectors in the following decades, during the so-called import-substitution industrialisation era (1945–1980).

Table 4.9 Poverty rate, 1913–1950 (%)

Country	*1913*	*1929*	*1938*	*1950*
Argentina	58	41	45	24
Chile	65	47	42	36
Colombia	90	70	65	61
Mexico	43	31	36	43

Source: Prados de la Escosura (2007)

4.4 The Mild Results in Welfare Progress

Despite the ambitious reforms aimed at enhancing the population's welfare, the standards of living saw more moderate improvement during the Liberal Republic era, compared to those of the take-off period (1914–1930). Living conditions continued to progress after 1930, but they did so at a slower pace than earlier in the twentieth century. The poverty rate declined to 65% and 61%, in 1938 and 1950 respectively, from 70% in 1929 (Prados de la Escosura, 2007). This was significant progress, but much more moderate than the 20% reduction observed in the three first decades of the twentieth century. Such differences can be observed in Table 4.9, where it can also be noted that poverty incidence remained higher than that of their Latin America peers by 1950.

Poverty decline has two drivers: economic growth and improvements in income distribution. The slow economic growth between 1930 and 1950 meant that Colombia's economy reduced its capacity to shift its inhabitants out of poverty. Likewise, the worsening in income inequality made harder poverty decline. The actual fact is that the Gini coefficient[3] rose to 45% and 51%, in 1938 and 1950, respectively, meaning that it was Colombians in the lower income bracket who bore the brunt of the consequences with regard to the economically turbulent period between 1930 and 1945. Indeed, Colombia never recovered its Gini level previously reached in 1929, perpetuating a high level of inequality which has remained up to the present day. If the economic growth driver lost power in reducing poverty, the income distribution driver completely vanished.

Despite the constraints the slowdown in poverty reduction and the rise of inequality, the HHDI saw an increase between 1930 and 1950 (see Table 4.10). In fact, the HHDI experienced an acceleration in its growth

[3] Gini coefficient taken from Prados de la Escosura (2007).

Table 4.10 Historical Human Development Index, 1920–1950

Year	*Argentina*	*Chile*	*Colombia*	*Mexico*
1920	0.58	0.43	0.33	0.33
1930	0.64	0.50	0.39	0.32
1940	0.68	0.51	0.44	0.39
1950	0.73	0.60	0.52	0.51

Source: Estimated based on MOxLAB (n.d.) for life expectancy and literacy, and Maddison Project Database for GDP per capita

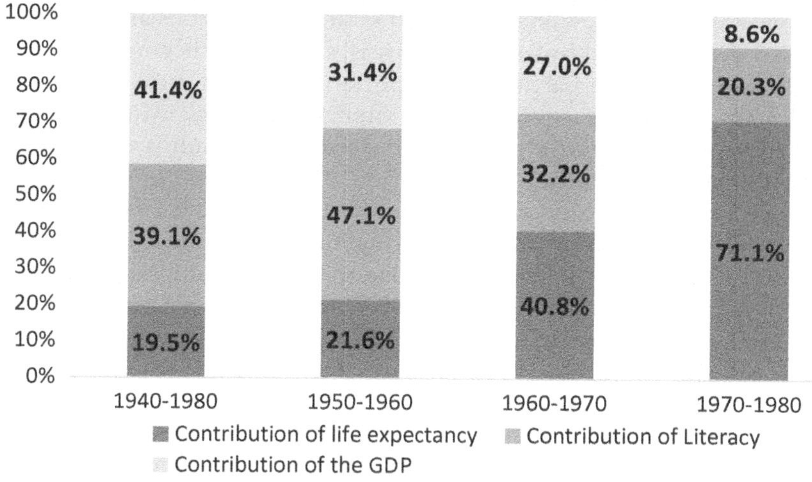

Fig. 4.4 Composition of HHDI, 1910–1950 (Source: Estimated based on MOxLAD (n.d.) for life expectancy and literacy, and Maddison Project Database for GDP per capita)

rate after 1940, indicating an acceleration in population welfare. How could the opposite trends between poverty and HHDI be reconciled? The answer lies in the driver(s) for the HHDI's growth, which after 1930 was mainly life expectancy (see Fig. 4.4). 71.1% of the HHDI's growth between 1940 and 1950 was due to an increase in life expectancy, while the GDP per capita only contributed 8.6%. That is very different from the cases throughout the 1910s and the 1920s, when the GDP per capita and literacy rate dominated the forces behind the HHDI's growth.

Between 1930 and 1950, Colombians saw moderate increases in their income and education levels, but they were now living longer. This extension to the population's average life span was certainly the main welfare accomplishment of the Liberal Republic era (1930–1945), although it was also a result of the material progress observed during the take-off period (1914–1929). The increase in life expectancy was a result of a decline in the mortality rate. Meisel, Ramirez, and Jaramillo (2018) estimated that the mortality rate declined to 13.2 deaths per 1000 inhabitants in 1951, from 30 in 1905. The article relates the massive decline in mortality rate to improvements in the fresh water supply and sewerage systems, which improved sanitary conditions and strongly reduced deaths caused by infectious diseases. The enhancements in sanitary conditions were particularly important in urban areas, which by 1951 had on average coverage rates higher than 60%. Much of that work was initiated during the take-off period, although it culminated and expanded after 1930.

Despite the slower economic growth between 1930 and 1945, an average Colombian person's standards of living improved, although this progress was mainly due to sanitary conditions, which allowed for a substantial rise in average life expectancy. In those 15 years, Colombia progressed in its demographic transition, in a period characterised by a heavy reduction in mortality rates and a rise in fertility. The increase in life expectancy was certainly important, and cannot be underestimated. The remaining question is, however, if such an improvement could have been even greater with higher economic growth rates than those reached during the 1920s. After 1930, Colombia's standards of living continued to progress, but the economic slowdown made that such welfare improvements were more moderate and less radical than that of the take-off period.

References

Avella, M. (2004). Antecedentes Históricos de la Deuda Colombiana. La Renegociación de la Deuda Externa de Colombia en los 1930 y 1940. Segunda Ronda: 1938–1942. *Borradores de Economía*, No. 293, Banco de la República.

Bergoeing, R., Kehoe, P., Kehoe, T., & Soto, R. (2002). Policy-Driven Productivity in Chile and Mexico in the 1980s and 1990s. *American Economic Review, 92*, 16–21.

Bushnell, D. (1993). *The Making of Modern Colombia: A Nation in Spite of Itself.* Berkeley and Los Angeles: University of California Press.

Cardenas, E. (2000). The Process of Accelerated Industrialization in Mexico, 1929–1982. In E. Cardenas, J. Ocampo, & R. Thorp (Eds.), *An Economic History of Twentieth-Century Latin America. Volume 3: Industrialization and the State in Latin America. The Postwar Years.* London: Palgrave Macmillan.

Junguito, R. (2018). *Cien Episodios de la Historia Económica de Colombia.* Bogota: Ariel.

Junguito, R., & Rincon, H. (2004). La Politica Fiscal en el siglo XX en Colombia. In M. Urrutia & E. Posada (Eds.), *Investigaciones recientes sobre historia económica colombiana.* Banco de la República Reportes del Emisor, No. 62.

Kalmanovitz, S. (2017). *Nueva Historia Económica de Colombia.* Bogota: Universidad Jorge Tadeo Lozano.

Maddison Project Database, Version 2018. Bolt, Jutta, Robert Inklaar, Herman de Jong and Jan Luiten van Zanden. (2018). *Rebasing 'Maddison': New Income Comparisons and the Shape of Long-Run Economic Development.* Retrieved from https://www.rug.nl/ggdc/historicaldevelopment/maddison/releases/maddison-project-database-2018

Meisel, A., Ramirez, M., & Jaramillo, J. (2018). Más de cien años de avances en el nivel de vida: El caso de Colombia. *Cuadernos de Historia Económica*, N.46. Banco de la Republica de Colombia.

Montenegro, S. (1982). La industria textil en Colombia: 1900–1945. *Desarrollo y Sociedad*, N.8, Universidad de los Andes.

MOxLAD. (n.d.). Montevideo-Oxford Latin America Economic History Database. Retrieved from http://moxlad.cienciassociales.edu.uy/

Ocampo, J. (2015). *Historia Económica de Colombia.* Bogota: Fondo de Cultura Económica.

Pachon, A., & Ramirez, M. T. (2006). *La Infraestructura de Transporte en Colombia Durante el Siglo XX.* Bogota: Fondo de Cultura Económica/Banco de la República.

Prados de la Escosura, L. (2007). Inequality and Poverty in Latin America: A Long-Run Exploration. In T. Hatton, K. O'Rourke, & A. Taylor (Eds.), *The New Comparative Economic History. Essays in Honor of Jeffrey G. Williamson.* Cambridge, MA: The MIT Press.

Urrutia, M., Pontón, A., & Posada, C. (2002). *El Crecimiento Económico Colombiano En El Siglo XX.* Bogotá: Fondo de Cultura Eonómica.

CHAPTER 5

The Import Substitution Era, 1945–1980: The Consolidation of Interventionism, Financial Repression, and the Slow Way to Industrialisation

Abstract Between 1945 and 1980, Colombia operated under the import-substitution industrialisation (ISI) framework. Protectionism against foreign trade and government intervention in the financial sector were the core of the ISI model in Colombia. In practicality, Central Bank assumed the new role of channelling resources from the financial sector to the government, state-owned companies, or favoured business.

Why did the economy not mobilise resources towards industry and trade sectors, where mass production technology could be better absorbed? The government's interventionism in credit allocation preferentially channelled resources towards sectors of low productivity such as agriculture, which ultimately slowed down the structural change. In the early 1970s, the government finally relaxed its interventionism, allowing the full adoption of mass production technology and an economic boom boosted by the industrial sector.

Keywords Import-substitution industrialisation • Financial repression • Structural change • Mass production • Urbanisation • Mexico

Between 1945 and 1980, Colombia, as did the other Latin America economies, operated under the import-substitution industrialisation framework. As was presented in Chap. 4, such a model was put into action in

I. Luzardo-Luna, *Colombia's Slow Economic Growth*,
Palgrave Studies in Economic History,
https://doi.org/10.1007/978-3-030-25755-2_5

the 1930s, but rather than a deliberate long-term plan, the protectionism policies were initially a response to the Great Depression of 1929. Such policies, however, instead be transitory, became permanent, and were even reinforced in the postwar period. Between 1945 and 1974, import-substitution industrialisation was widely accepted by the Colombian elite as a dogma. During this period, Colombia experienced different ideological governments: Conservative, Liberal, and even a military dictatorship. All of them, however, followed the import-substitution industrialisation model.

Protectionism against foreign trade and strong government intervention in the financial sector were the core of the import-substitution industrialisation model in Colombia. Unlike several countries in Latin America, Colombia followed a relatively orthodox management of fiscal and monetary policies, which prevented the country from going through episodes of debt crisis or hyperinflation. Such a combination of interventionism, protectionism, and orthodox management led to slow, but stable, economic growth. Figure 5.1 presents the real GDP per capita for Argentina, Chile, Colombia, and Mexico between 1945 and 1980. Colombia's economy did not see the strong fluctuations observed in Argentina and Chile, but grew more slowly and, in 1960, was overtaken by Mexico. This latter

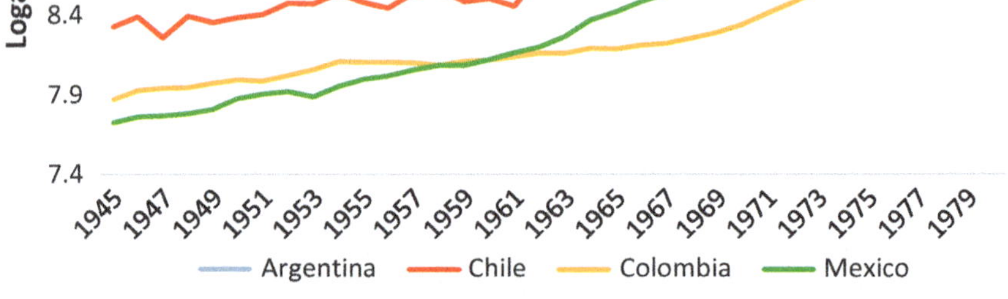

Fig. 5.1 Real GDP per capita at 2011 US$ prices (logs), 1945–1980 (Source: Maddison Project Database, Version 2018. Bolt, Jutta, Robert Inklaar, Herman de Jong and Jan Luiten van Zanden (2018))

country showed the best economic performance in Latin America during that period, as it was the only one which developed a world-class industrial sector able to compete in the world economy. Mexico, unlike Colombia, was able to fully absorb mass consumption technology and it was this that propelled its growth up to the 1980s debt crisis, although this process started in the 1930s, as was discussed in Chap. 4.

5.1 Violence, Industrialisation, and the Consolidation of Interventionism, 1946–1958

In 1946, the Liberal Republic came to an end, as the Conservative candidate, Mariano Ospina Pérez, won the presidential elections. In general terms, the new Conservative administration shared the belief that the government should have a more active role in the management of the economy, and this included the protection of the rising industrial sector from international competition. There were, however, some political circumstances that finally pushed the government into taking action with protectionist measurements against international trade.

On 9 April 1948, the Liberal leader Jorge Eliécer Gaitán was assassinated, and this initiated a bloody conflict known as *La Violencia* (The Violence). Unlike the civil wars of the nineteenth century, *La Violencia* was a non-declared war between the Liberal and Conservative parties, which was fought by paramilitary forces on each side in rural areas. The consequences of the violent conflict, which lasted until 1958, were terrible in terms of the loss of life and political instability.

During the turbulent environment that existed in June 1948, the government established a new import tax, with rates between 10% and 25%, known as *Impuesto de Giro* (Ocampo, 2015, p. 243). Such a measure deteriorated the country's commercial relationship with the United States, which in 1949 terminated the trade agreement that had been in force since 1935 (Ocampo, 2015, p. 243). This decision did not prevent Colombia from continuing to export to the United States, but probably had a negative impact on the diversification of exports. Coffee remained as Colombia's main source of 'hard currency', and accounted for more than 70% of exports between 1945 and 1958.

The assassination of Gaitán led to major and violent riots in Bogota, in the so-called *El Bogotazo*. The magnitude of the unrest was very intense.

Banks, shops, and even government buildings were looted and destroyed by mobs of rioters. To support the reconstruction of affected business, the government issued Decree-Law 1407 of 1948, increasing the Central Bank's lending capacity and its financial regulatory role. Such measurements, which were reinforced with the financial reform of 1951 (Ocampo, 2015), established caps on the interest rates of the Commercial Bank, discretionary power on the bank's reserve ratio, and special credit lines to support agricultural and industrial development. The changes in the Central Bank's role meant its consolidation as a developing bank. In practicality, the new role of the Central Bank was to channel resources from the financial sector to the government, state-owned companies, or favoured business. The 1948 and 1951 reforms were the beginning of the *financial repression* model, which operated up to 1974, and consisted of funding the government via financial sector regulation.

Under the scheme of protectionism and interventionism in the financial sector, Colombia's economy continued to operate throughout the import-substitution period. As the country moved closer to the world economy, exports reduced in significance, and their share with regard to the GDP reduced to 17.2% in 1958, from 22.6% in 1946 (Urrutia, Pontón, & Posada, 2002). Although international coffee prices remained its influence on the business cycle, the domestic market consolidated as the main force behind economic performance.

The economic growth between 1946 and 1958 was higher than that of the Liberal Republic (see Table 5.1), but it relied more on capital, and less on the TFP. The latter, however, saw a significant increase of up to 1.84% from the 1.41% reached by the Liberal Republic. In other words, despite there being an acceleration in productivity gains after 1945, the economy now depended more on investment.

Table 5.1 Accountability of the GDP growth, 1905–1999 (%)

Period	*GDP growth*	*Contribution of capital*	*Contribution of labour force*	*TFP*
1905–1929	5.75	0.71	1.13	3.92
1930–1945	3.46	0.88	1.18	1.41
1946–1958	4.74	1.82	1.07	1.84
1959–1980	5.31	1.94	1.59	1.78
1905–1996	4.74	1.40	1.43	1.90

Source: Urrutia et al. (2002)

The source of the increase in productivity for the Colombian economy in the early postwar period was the greater absorption rate of mass production technology. What laid behind that process was a structural change, which meant a relative decline in the agriculture sector and an increase for industry. In other words, Colombia was mobilising resources from a sector of low productivity (agriculture) towards one of high productivity (industry) (see Table 5.4). The difference in productivity between the two sectors lies in the fact that the latter used mass production technology more intensely.

The path towards industrialisation in Colombia was, however, slow. Table 5.2 shows that in 1950, agriculture still accounted for 38.2% of Colombia's GDP, a share substantially higher than that of Mexico. The difference between the two countries reveals the accelerated industrialisation of Mexico during the 1930s and the Second World War, which also increased the size of its commerce and finance sectors. In fact, in this latter sector, the gap between Colombia and Mexico in 1950 was even higher in the case of industry. Despite its relatively low share, Colombia's industry grew substantially in the 1950s and approached the level of Mexico in 1958. Such expansion meant a decline in the agricultural sector, which is related to the reduction of the rural population.

Table 5.2 Composition of the GDP by economic sector, real GDP per capita at 2011 US$ prices (logs), 1950–1958 (%)

Sector	*1950*		*1955*		*1958*	
	Colombia	*Mexico*	*Colombia*	*Mexico*	*Colombia*	*Mexico*
Agriculture	38.2	19.2	33.8	18.7	35.1	17.4
Mining	3.5	5.0	3.4	4.8	3.6	4.8
Industry	14.8	17.1	16.1	17.5	17.4	18.1
Electricity, gas, and water	0.5	0.7	0.6	0.9	0.7	0.9
Construction	2.7	3.6	3.7	3.7	3.2	3.9
Commerce, finances, and other services	22.6	31.6	23.6	31.2	21.8	31.0
Transportation and communication	5.4	3.3	7.0	3.5	6.0	3.5
Government, social, and personal services	12.3	19.5	11.9	19.7	12.2	20.4
Total	100	100	100	100	100	100

Source: ECLAC National Accounts Database (n.d.)

In the 1950s, Colombia saw accelerated urbanisation, which was fuelled by the intensity of rural violence. *La violencia* forced thousands of peasants to leave the countryside and migrate to the cities. In 1950, Colombia's urbanisation was only 35% (Prados de la Escosura, 2007), which meant that the country was still mainly rural. Ten years later, in 1960, this proportion increased up to 48%, becoming the country in Latin America with the highest growth in urbanisation in that decade (Prados de la Escosura, 2007).

Colombia's political elite remained engaged in profound polarisation in the early 1950s, which ended in a *coup d'état* in 1953 which initiated five years of military dictatorship up to 1958. Under the dictatorship, the confrontation between the political parties declined, but it rose between the military government and irregular armed groups. As in its early phase in the aftermath of *el Bogotazo*, the conflict was concentrated in rural areas, but with higher intensity, which is what led to the migration of more peasants to urban settings. According to Kalmanovitz, 2017, p. 315), the rate of homicide increased in the second half of the 1950s, which would indicate an exacerbation of violence, thus boosting internal migration.

The new labour force arriving to the cities could not be completely absorbed by industry, and this generated unemployment and underemployment in the low productivity services (Ocampo, 2015, p. 236). In other words, the unexpected and rapid internal migration led a share of the labour force towards the so-called *informal economy*, which is characterised by operating in low productivity services. This segment of the economy expanded throughout the 1950s, and it is plausible to assume that it could have had a negative impact on aggregate labour productivity. Between 1950 and 1958, Colombia's labour productivity, measured as output per hour worked expanded, but from 1954, it did so at a slower pace (see Fig. 5.2). The opposite was the case for Mexico, which continued to expand its productivity in the industrial sector.

Apart from the problem of underemployment, another reason for labour productivity growth slowing down from 1954 was stagnation in structural change. The agricultural sector was still very large in 1955, and it increased its share on the value added in 1958. The natural transition, which meant the mobilisation of resources from agriculture towards industry and services, was interrupted in the middle of the 1950s. This slowdown was probably influenced by the government's increasing role in credit allocation towards favoured sectors. Such capacity was strengthened with the financial reform of 1951, which by the Decree

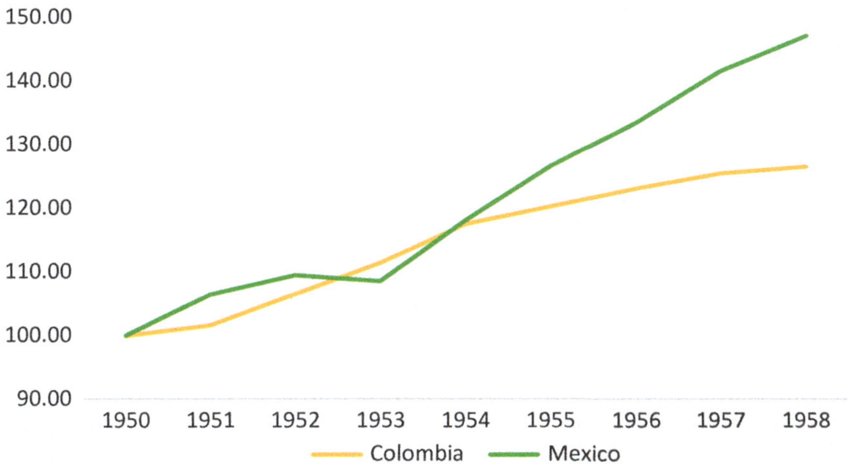

Fig. 5.2 Index of real labour productivity (output per hour worked), 1950–1958 (1950 = 100) (Source: Estimated based on Timmer, de Vries, & de Vries, 2015)

2314 of 1953 established the *Banco Cafetero* (Coffee Bank). The entity, ruled by Fedecafe, had as its main purpose to support coffee, and other agricultural goods, production and exportation. The government continued channelling resources towards the coffee sector and restricted to the rest of the economy.

5.2 Political Consensus, Higher Doses of Interventionism, and Low Productivity Services, 1958–1974

In 1958, Colombia returned to democracy, as a consequence of a political agreement between the Liberal and Conservative parties known as the *Frente Nacional* (National Front). In the late 1950s and early 1960s, the import-substitution industrialisation view, which emerged as an unplanned policy response during the Great Depression of 1929, was theoretically formalised by the so-called Economic Commission of Latin America—ECLA's school. The economists behind this theory strongly supported import-substitution industrialisation, as they forecast a deterioration in the exchange terms against commodities goods in the long run. In this case, if the Latin American economies remained oriented towards exporting commodities and importing industrial goods, they would only have perpetuated a dependence relationship with other developed countries. This dependence relationship was seen as the fundamental reason for Latin American underdevelopment. It is from such an economic view that the reasons can be understood for the strong economic efforts in promoting the industrial sector, with even more protectionist policies, and other forms of interventionism.

ECLA's school was correct in that economic growth at that time passed by the acceleration of the transition from economies based on commodities towards industrial goods. That was the way in which mass production technology could have been utilised to the highest degree. The policy recommendations, however, worked in the opposite direction as protectionism and interventionism certainly slowed down industrialisation. ECLA's theorists probably did not consider the political economy of the government's resources allocation, and the relatively high power of some sectors in agriculture to harvest such resources. In the case of Colombia, the increase in the government's discretionary power for resource allocation actually moved in the opposite direction to what was envisaged by ECLA's theory. The actual fact is that due to the strong influence of the coffee sector, the increase in government interventionism finally resulted in resource mobilisation towards coffee producers, and other favoured sectors, and away from the rest of the economy.

ECLA's theory did not anticipate the perverse incentives that protectionism created on the protected industrial sector either. Due to a lack of competence, several domestic industries became monopolies or oligopolies, with few incentives for innovation or exportation being profitable only through the dominant positions they held in their own domestic markets. Likewise, protectionism increased the cost of importing, which included machinery and capital goods, which inevitably had a negative effect on productivity.

Between 1959 and 1980, Colombia's economic growth accelerated compared with the period 1945–1958. This increase in economic growth, however, was driven by a substantial increase in the labour force (Table 5.1). While capital accumulation saw mild acceleration, the TFP moderate its growth. In other words, the acceleration of the economic growth in the 1960s was due to the economy at that time being able to incorporate more workers into its production capacity.

Table 5.3 Composition of the GDP by economic sector, real GDP per capita at 2011 US$ prices (logs), 1960–1979 (%)

Sector	*1960*		*1970*		*1979*	
	Colombia	*Mexico*	*Colombia*	*Mexico*	*Colombia*	*Mexico*
Agriculture	32.98	17.2	25.1	12.1	21.5	9.2
Mining, construction, electricity, water, and gas	7.68	10.8	7.0	8.6	7.1	10.0
Industry	17.86	20.8	20.7	22.0	22.5	21.1
Services and government	41.48	51.2	4	57.3	49.0	59.6

Source: Estimated based on Timmer et al. (2015)

The drivers behind higher labour force growth rates were urbanisation, high birth rates in the 1940s and the 1950s, and more intense incorporation of women into the labour market. Such demographic changes were not followed by an increase in productivity growth due to a slow structural change. The share of agriculture with regard to GDP was still very large in 1970, relative to that of Mexico, which constrained a quicker absorption of mass technology. This ‘technological wave’, however, had the potential to be incorporated not only into industry, but also into the services sector (Table 5.3).

The fast and traumatic urbanisation of Colombia avoided that the industrial sector could absorb many of the city’s newcomers, who went to work in services of low productivity. In 1980, the share of the employed population working in the trade[1] sector reached 18%, from a rate of 4.9% in 1950. Many of these workers were migrants from the countryside working in the cities as street vendors, in corner shops, and other atomised trades with very low levels of productivity. Table 5.4 shows relative labour productivity by sector for Colombia and Mexico. While in 1950, the relative productivity of the trade sector was 470% of the total economy average, in 1980, this indicator fell to just 120%. Colombia not only had problems absorbing mass distribution technology into industry, but also into service. As important as the slow incorporation of mass production, in the 1960s, Colombia was facing a problem of slow embracement of mass distribution technology.

The importance of productivity growth in the service industry was noted by Broadberry (1997). The author maintains that the main reason

[1] Including restaurants and hotels.

Table 5.4 Relative labour productivity by sector for Colombia and Mexico, 1950–1980 (%)

Productivity	*1950*	*1960*	*1970*	*1980*
Agriculture	0.4	0.3	0.3	0.3
Mining	0.1	0.1	0.2	0.2
Manufacturing	1.1	1.0	1.1	1.5
Utilities	3.7	3.4	3.9	3.5
Construction	1.8	1.4	1.1	1.5
Trade, restaurants, and hotels	4.5	3.4	1.9	1.2
Transport, storage, and communication	0.7	0.8	0.6	0.9
Finance, insurance, real estate, and business services	2.1	1.3	1.2	0.8
Community, social, and personal services	0.6	0.6	0.5	0.5
Summation of sector GDP	1	1	1	1

Source: Estimated based on Timmer et al. (2015)

why the United States overtook Britain in terms of overall productivity was the higher productivity growth rate of American services during the interwar period. In the case of Colombia, trade saw productivity decline between 1950 and 1980 due to the fragmented nature in which this sector developed in this period, which led to many outlets of low value being added. In fact, Colombia had to wait until the 1990s in order to see actual national retail chains.

Despite its relative decline during the import substitution era, in 1950, the labour productivity of the trade sector was 4.5 times higher than the economy average. In this case, why did the economy not mobilise resources towards this sector? Here, financial repression, or the government's interventionism in credit allocation and interest rates, played a significant role. With such controls, the government preferentially channelled resources towards sectors of low productivity such as agriculture over sectors of high productivity, as was described in Eq. 4.2 in Chap. 4. Despite the high potential for growth due to accelerated urbanisation, the lack of the financial sector being able to allocate capital where it could have reached the highest possible return, led to slow productivity expansion. Throughout the import-substitution era, credit grew and had the potential to propel economic growth. The government's excessive intervention, however, prevent from the credit resources mobilisation toward where they could gain a higher return profitability, which ultimately slowed down the chances for structural change, and therefore economic growth.

5.3 Policy Adjustments and the End of the Imports Substitution Era, 1974–1980

In 1974, the *Frente National* agreement came to an end, and Colombia moved towards a competitive elections framework. That year, the Liberal candidate Alfonso López Michelsen, the son of President Alfonso López Pumarejo, won the presidential elections. From 1970 onward, inflation started to accelerate, and in 1973 it reached 23.5%. This fact was noted and strongly criticised by López Michelsen as the opposition leader, which put forward excessive fiscal deficit as the main reason behind the acceleration in the rate of inflation (Ocampo, 2015, p. 252). Once in power, the new administration made as its main priority the reduction of the fiscal deficit, which was essential in fixing the financial sector, as the government's interventionism in credit allocation was the main driver behind the high level of public spending.

In 1974, the government introduced a financial reform, which eliminated the forced investments that private companies had to make in the Central Bank. It also reduced the reserve ratio and increased interest rates (Ocampo, 2015, p. 252). The reform also reduced the Central Bank's role as a development bank, but it did not completely eliminate it. That would only occur in 1991 with the new constitution. The reform was one step towards the liberalisation of the financial market, but the government retained a significant role with regard to credit allocation through the large public-owned companies, which were the main players in the mining, communication, and energy sectors.

The López Michelsen administration was successful in eliminating fiscal deficit, and the government balance showed its first surplus since 1975. Such orthodox fiscal policy allowed a substantial reduction of external debt up to 1979, which was a fundamental basis for debt crisis management in the early 1980s. Likewise, the improvements in credit allocation allowed for an increase in industrial labour productivity (see Table 5.5), but it did not have the same effect on trade. The latter is probably related to the fact that urbanisation continued to grow in the 1970s. According to World Bank statistics, in 1980, urbanisation rates reached 63.7%, up from 56.6% that was observed in 1970. The economy certainly struggled to integrate the high share of the labour force, which remained working in the so-called informal economy.

The improvements in labour productivity in the industrial sector could be observed by looking at exports. In 1980, industrial exports accounted

Table 5.5 Index of real labour productivity growth, 1950–1980 (1950 = 100)

Productivity	*1950*	*1960*	*1970*	*1980*
Agriculture	100	140	223	238
Mining	100	177	566	718
Manufacturing	100	168	251	434
Utilities	100	176	266	303
Construction	100	149	158	270
Trade, restaurants, and hotels	100	148	111	84
Transport, storage, and communication	100	220	237	407
Finance, insurance, real estate, and business services	100	126	146	129
Community, social, and personal services	100	191	210	272
All sectors	100	196	257	322

Source: Estimated based on Timmer et al. (2015)

for 23%[2] of total exports, a share significantly higher than the 12% reached in 1970. Behind such growth, there was outstanding growth in clothing, processed food, chemical, and metal industries. All of this occurred at the same time that the government reduced its protectionist measures. In 1973, the average tariff was reduced to 48.5% (Ocampo, 2015, p. 253)—still high, but lower than the 65.6% observed in 1964. This reduction probably facilitated the importation of machinery and other capital goods, which was needed to increase industrial productivity.

In the 1970s, Colombia finally witnessed industrial goods being exported on a significant scale, but as was the case for the railways, the country embraced mass production technology very late. Again, the late arrival to this second wave of general purpose technology was the key factor behind Colombia's slow growth between the years of 1930 and 1970. Colombia could only properly embark on the mass production revolution in the 1970s, when the industrial sector moved beyond the national market and was able to export. In the late 1980s, the world economy moved towards a new technological wave with the arrival of commercial Internet, and the enabling general purpose technology then became ICTs, rather than mass production. In that sense, the window of opportunity to reach development through industrialisation narrowed. The actual fact is that Colombia only began to fully exploit the possibilities of mass production in the 1970s, and not in the 1930s as did Mexico, which limited the benefits of such technological wave.

[2] Source: Urrutia et al. (2002).

5.4 The Boom of the 1970s, and the Improvement in the Standard of Living

In the second half of the twentieth century, Colombia accelerated its welfare improvements. This fact can be noted in the poverty rates estimated by Prados de la Escosura (2007), which reduced its levels to 32% by 1980, from a previous 61% in 1950 (see Table 5.6). According to this estimation, for the first time in Colombian history, more than the half of the population were living out of poverty, which was certainly a major accomplishment. It is worth noting, however, that such enhancements in the standards of living were not equally distributed during the entire import substitution period. The actual fact is that poverty mainly reduced between 1970 and 1980, when it saw a decline of more than 20%. Such a tremendous reduction was a result of an upturn in the economy, and improvements in income distribution in that decade.

The two drivers for poverty reduction—economic growth and income distribution—underwent substantial improvements in the 1970s. The Gini index declined more than eight points, to reach a level of 48.8% in 1980 from 57.3% in 1970. This fact indicates that faster economic growth was spreading towards the lower income bracket citizens. As was previously stated, the main driver was the more rapid economic growth in 1970 when there was a wider incorporation of mass production technology into the economy's production capacity, which allowed for the transition of a substantial share of the labour force to migrate from agriculture towards industry and services. The growing demand for unskilled workers in a surging industrial sector was the main mechanism in which the benefits of economic growth and mass production technology reached the lower income groups, leading to the improvement in income distribution. The wider adoption of mass production technology also benefitted the population through consumption, by increasing the availability of products, at

Table 5.6 Poverty rate, 1950–1990 (%)

Country	*1950*	*1960*	*1970*	*1980*	*1990*
Argentina	24	22	10	11	17
Chile	36	36	28	31	29
Colombia	61	57	52	32	37
Mexico	43	41	27	13	15

Source: Prados de la Escosura (2007)

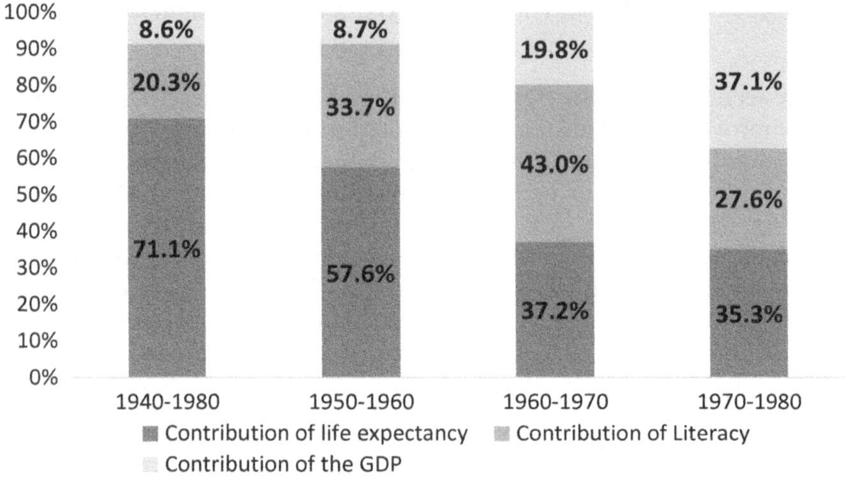

Fig. 5.3 Drivers of the HHDI, 1940–1980 (Source: Estimated based on MOxLAD (n.d.) for life expectancy and literacy, and Maddison Project Database for GDP per capita)

more affordable prices. A good example of this fact is the development of the poultry industry which saw a major increase in productivity in the 1970s (Galvis, 2000), increasing the intake of protein for the population.

The 1970s also saw a major improvement in the HHDI, which increased to 0.73 in 1980 from 0.66 in 1970. This important growth, however, was consistent with the behaviour throughout the entire twentieth century. In fact, the growth of the HHDI accelerated between 1940 and 1980 (see Fig. 5.3), although the drivers for this growth did not have the same impact during these four decades. As was discussed in Chap. 4, the main driver for the HHDI during the 1940s was the increase in average life expectancy. In the 1950s, life expectancy remained as the HHDI's main driver, but literacy rates also strengthened its impact. The pattern of change was reinforced in the 1960s, when literacy became the main driver for HHDI growth (Table 5.7).

After 1950, Colombia saw a rise in mass schooling, with a huge increase in the number of pupils, teachers, and schools (Ramirez & Tellez, 2007). This transformation was strongly influenced by the increase in public expenditure, including local governments, on education and urbanisation. By 1970, Colombia reached a primary school enrolment rate of 100% for

Table 5.7 HHDI, 1940–1980

Year	*Argentina*	*Chile*	*Colombia*	*Mexico*
1940	0.68	0.51	0.44	0.39
1950	0.73	0.60	0.52	0.51
1960	0.77	0.67	0.60	0.58
1970	0.80	0.73	0.66	0.67
1980	0.83	0.78	0.73	0.76

Source: Estimated based on MOxLAB (n.d.) for life expectancy and literacy, and Maddison Project Database for GDP per capita

the population sector between 7 and 11 years old, when in 1951, the rate was only 54.5% (Ramirez & Tellez, 2007).

In the 1970s, the main driver for improvements in the HHDI was economic growth, a phenomenon not seen since the take-off period (1900–1929). Between 1970 and 1978, the GDP per capita grew at an annual average of 5.5%, certainly higher than the average observed after 1930, which meant an acceleration in economic growth compared to the import substitution era standards. Why did economic growth only pick up in the 1970s and not before? Does the good economic performance in the 1970s validate the import-substitution strategy, despite the slow economic growth between 1930 and the late 1960s? To address these questions, again, it is useful to analyse the drivers for economic growth.

Table 5.8 shows the drivers for economic and industrial growth between 1950 and 1980. The main driver for economic growth in the 1970s was labour, which accounted for almost half the economic growth during this decade. The reason that the economy picked up in the 1970s was because it was able to incorporate more workers into its production capacity. On the other hand, industrial production's fast growth in the 1970s was mainly due to capital growth, which highlights an acceleration in investment in this sector.

The rapid and somewhat traumatic urbanisation of Colombian led to peasants being rendered as urban unemployed individuals. The slow economic growth and lower educational levels in the countryside made the task of finding a job hard for many of the newcomers. The rate of unemployment rose to 12.3% in 1967 from 5.1% in 1958, when the economy was essentially at 'full employment'. As can be observed in Fig. 5.4, unemployment reached its peak in the late 1960s, then saw a substantial decline up to, and including, the late 1970s. Likewise, the rate of labour force

Table 5.8 Drivers of industrial and economic growth, 1950–1980 (%)

Year	*Total economy*				*Industrial sector*			
	Economic Growth	*Contribution of technological change*	*Contribution of labour*	*Contribution of capital*	*Production Growth*	*Contribution of technological change*	*Contribution of labour*	*Contribution of capital*
1940–1949	4.3	2.1	1.0	1.2	8.6	4.0	2.2	2.4
1950–1959	5.3	2.2	1.3	1.7	7.1	1.9	2.7	3.9
1960–1969	5.1	1.5	1.5	2.0	5.8	5.0	0.8	2.7
1970–1979	5.7	0.5	2.8	2.4	6.5	3.2	1.9	3.5

Source: Echavarria and Villamizar (2007)

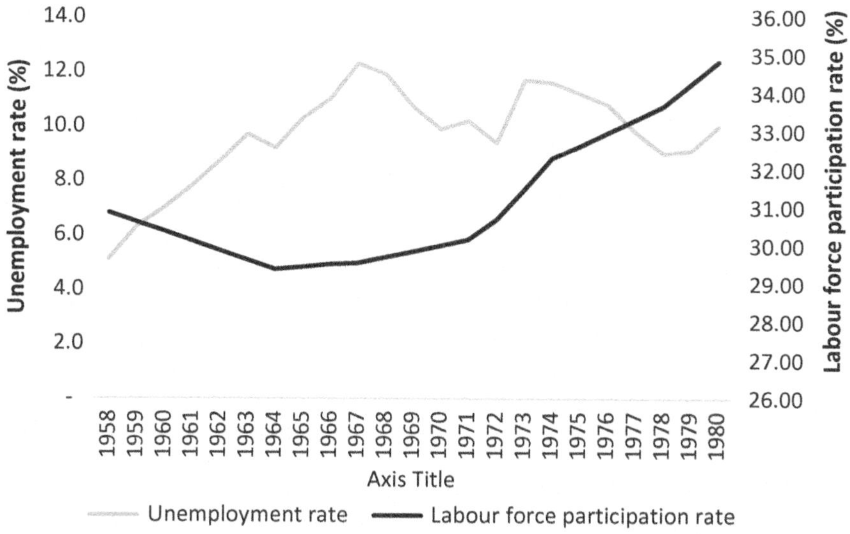

Fig. 5.4 Unemployment and labour force participation rate, 1958–1980 (%) (Source: Londoño, 1995)

participation increased to 34.8% in 1980 from 29.5% in 1967. The decline in unemployment along with the increase in the labour participation rate meant a substantial increase in the employed population, which boosted the aggregate production functions. In other words, the strong economic growth of the 1970s was essentially a labour input-driven growth, where more available workers led to a higher output.

Many of these new workers went to work in industry, although the distribution was relatively even between non-agricultural sectors, with services also accounting for a significant share. By 1973, the share of employees working in large industrial firms was 12.1%—higher than the 10.8% average observed in the 1960s (Londoño, 1995, p. 227). Without doubt, the industrial sector was the driver for the economic boom that took place in the 1970s, as this sector was able to absorb an increasing share of skilled workers, which arose from the surge in mass schooling in the 1950s. Mass production technology was finally spreading at a pace that made Colombia's industry competitive enough to generate industrial exports, and not only rely on the domestic market as had previously been the case.

The rapid growth of the industrial sector led to an increase in the hiring of new workers, which increased the working population, and this ultimately propelled Colombia's economic growth. In other words, the good economic performance of the 1970s was to a large extent the result of the acceleration of the industrial sector, which by that decade, was strongly embracing mass production technology, increasing the significance of industrial employment. The results presented in Table 5.8 maintain that the driver for the accelerated industrial expansion was a combination of accumulated capital and productivity growth. Industrial investment picked up in the 1970s, but unlike the 1950s, it did so in a way that significantly increased its productivity, indicating a substantial technological change. The general purpose technology that explains such an important surge in productivity was mass production.

The key element behind the high economic growth rates of the 1970s was the acceleration in industrial investment. At this point, the importance of banking, and the negative effects of financial repression became evident. Table 5.9 shows the sources of funding for industrial companies between 1950 and 1978. Up to the mid-1960s, industrial firms were funded mainly by internal sources, which was both retained earnings and capital contributions. Even if in the 1960s loans increased the contribution, their share remained below 50%. In the early 1970s, there was a substantial increase in the participation of loans as a source of funding for industrial firms, which was reinforced between the years of 1976–1978. In the 1970s, there was a notable increase in credit available to industry, and this certainly facilitated the industrial firms' financial leverage.

The relevance of the mobilisation of credit towards production activities has been widely discussed in the literature of economic history (Echavarria & Villamizar, 2007; Levine, 2005; Rajan & Zingales, 1998).

Table 5.9 Source of funding for industrial sector, 1950–1978 (%)

Period	*Retained earnings*	*Capital contribution*	*Loans*	*Total*
1950–1954	39.1	33.5	27.4	100
1955–1959	41.1	33.1	25.8	100
1960–1964	30.1	27.8	42.1	100
1965–1969	47.9	9.9	42.2	100
1970–1974	46.8	6.5	46.7	100
1976–1978	36.6	4.8	58.6	100

Source: Echavarria and Villamizar (2007)

In the case of Colombia, the poor development of its financial market was a result of the government's financial repression policies and its active interventionism, which prioritised funding for public administrations, and the allocation of credit to firms that were suffering from substantial losses, over the development of a financial market. The financial reforms of 1974, which eliminated the forced investment in the Central Bank, loosened the level of financial repression, allowing for a higher flow of resources towards the industrial sector as well as the rest of the economy (see Fig. 5.5). Despite these reforms being a step in the right direction, Colombia's share of domestic credit to the private sector in the 1970s was lower than that of South Korea, which witnessed rapid progress towards industrialisation during the same period. In fact, South Korea had a lower ratio of domestic credit to its GDP than Colombia in the early 1960s, but it experienced outstanding growth in 1966 (see Fig. 5.5). Despite their limitations, the financial reforms undertaken under President López Michelsen's administration, which contributed to relieving financial repression, was one of the ultimate reasons behind the economic boom in the 1970s. As the financial reforms were only implemented in 1974, their benefits only materialised

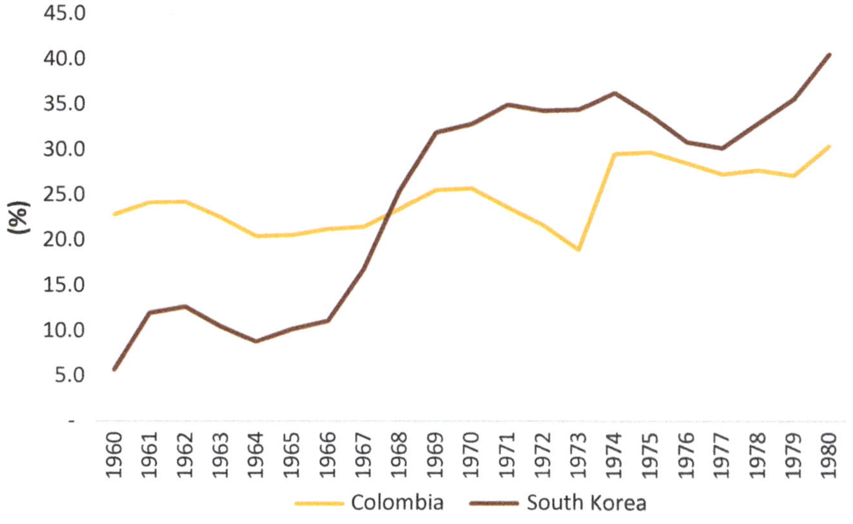

Fig. 5.5 Domestic credit to private sector, 1960–1980 (% of GDP) (Source: World Bank, Global Development Data, n.d.)

in the second half of the 1970s. The successful economic performance in the early 1970s is explained by two other elements: external credit and being relieved of protectionism.

By the early 1970s, private external debt had grown and it reached $1.038 billion in 1974, from only $457 million in 1970 (Garay, 1991). This increase was due, to a large extent, to the result of the increased availability of resources in international capital markets that were looking for high returns in developing countries. There is no precise estimation of how much external credit was allocated to the different sectors for these years, but Garay (1991, p. 606) estimated that, on average, the industrial sector accounted for 50% of the private debt balance between 1978 and 1982, which is why it is plausible to assume that a substantial share of the loans contracted in the early 1970s went to manufacturing companies. The greater access to international loans explains in part the rapid growth in investment in the industrial sector in the early 1970s. Within the credit allocated to the industrial sector, Garay (1991, p. 607) highlights the importance of the textile and clothing industries, where three major companies accounted for 13.5% of private external debt by March 1984. This fact explains the dynamism, the dynamism of clothing exportation in that, by 1970, it accounted for just 1% of industrial exports, but by 1979 it had reached a level of 14%.

The boom in industrial exports in the 1970s was also favoured by the relief of protectionism, as well as a new exchange rate policy that had been in force since 1967, known as the 'crawling peg', which permitted small daily devaluations. Likewise, tariff reductions fostered the input from imports, which were required by the industrial sector to operate effectively. Imports increased to US$4.7 billion in 1980, from only $843 million in 1970. Most of these imports were either capital goods or inputs, as consumption goods accounted for less than 15% of the value for imports during the 1970s.

In general terms, the good economic and social results of the 1970s are explained by the relief of protectionism and financial repression. Relaxed government interventionism finally allowed the full adoption of mass production technology, which had been available since the 1930s, but Colombia did not fulfil the economic pre-conditions to embrace this new technological wave. Once credit and inputs finally flowed towards the industrial sector, there was a genuine increase in industrial production and exportation, and this generated the sources that allowed the substantial improvement in the standards of living.

By 1980, Colombia's economy seemed to be in a virtuous cycle of fast economic growth, improvements in the standards of living, and a decline in income inequality. Unfortunately, this golden decade was followed by a long-lasting period of stagnation—that lasted 20 years—where the country faced severe economic crises and a new surge of violence that worsened the standards of living between 1980 and 2000. Two negative shocks severely impacted Colombia's economy in the last two decades of the twentieth century: the violence generated by the war against drugs, and the Latin American debt crisis of the 1980s. Besides important shocks, the structural reason behind Colombia's poor economic performance remained the excessive government interventionism in the allocation of resources. The path initiated towards economic liberalisation in the early 1970s ceased in 1978, and would only resume in the early 1990s.

References

Broadberry, S. (1997). How Did the United States and Germany Overtake Britain? A Sectoral Analysis of Comparative Productivity Levels, 1870–1990. *The Journal of Economic History, 58*, 375–407.

Echavarria, J., & Villamizar, M. (2007). El proceso Colombiano de desindustrialización. In M. Urrutia & J. Robinson (Eds.), *Economía colombiana del siglo XX: un análisis cuantitativo*. Bogota: Fondo de Cultura Económica.

Economic Commission for Latin America and the Caribbean ECLAC. (n.d.) National Accounts Database. Retrieved from https://estadisticas.cepal.org/cepalstat/Portada.html

Galvis, L. (2000). *La demanda de carnes en Colombia: Un análisis econométrico. Documentos de trabajo sobre economía regional.* Cartagena: Banco de La Republica.

Garay, L. (1991). *Colombia y la crisis de la deuda*. Bogota: CINEP and Universidad Nacional.

Kalmanovitz, S. (2017). *Nueva Historia Económica de Colombia*. Bogota: Universidad Jorge Tadeo Lozano.

Levine, R. (2005). Finance and Growth: Theory and Evidence. In Ph. Aghion & S. Durlauf (Eds.), *Handbook of Economic Growth* (Ed. 1, Vol. 1, Chap. 12, pp. 865–934). Elsevier. https://doi.org/10.1016/S1574-0684(05)01012-9

Londoño, J. (1995). *Distribución del Ingreso y Desarrollo Económico: Colombia en el siglo XX*. Bogota: Tercer Milenio.

Maddison Project Database, Version 2018. Bolt, Jutta, Robert Inklaar, Herman de Jong and Jan Luiten van Zanden. (2018). *Rebasing 'Maddison': New Income Comparisons and the Shape of Long-Run Economic Development*. Retrieved from https://www.rug.nl/ggdc/historicaldevelopment/maddison/releases/maddison-project-database-2018

MOxLAD. (n.d.). Montevideo-Oxford Latin America Economic History Database. Retrieved from http://moxlad.cienciassociales.edu.uy/

Ocampo, J. (2015). *Historia Económica de Colombia*. Bogota: Fondo de Cultura Económica.

Prados de la Escosura, L. (2007). Inequality and Poverty in Latin America: A Long-Run Exploration. In T. Hatton, K. O'Rourke, & A. Taylor (Eds.), *The New Comparative Economic History. Essays in Honor of Jeffrey G. Williamson*. Cambridge, MA: The MIT Press.

Rajan, R., & Zingales, L. (1998). Financial Dependence and Growth. *American Economic Review, 88*(3), 559–586.

Ramirez, M., & Tellez, J. (2007). La educación primaria y secundaria en Colombia en el siglo XX. In M. Urrutia & J. Robinson (Eds.), *Economía colombiana del siglo XX: un análisis cuantitativo*. Bogotá: Fondo de Cultura Económica.

Timmer, M. P., de Vries, G. J., & de Vries, K. (2015). Patterns of Structural Change in Developing Countries. In J. Weiss & M. Tribe (Eds.), *Routledge Handbook of Industry and Development* (pp. 65–83). London: Routledge. Retrieved from https://www.rug.nl/ggdc/productivity/10-sector/

Urrutia, M., Pontón, A., & Posada, C. (2002). *El Crecimiento Económico Colombiano En El Siglo XX*. Bogotá: Fondo de Cultura Eonómica.

World Bank, Global Development Data. (n.d.). Retrieved from https://data.worldbank.org/

CHAPTER 6

The Lost Decades, 1980–2000: External Debt, Structural Reforms, and a Deep Financial Crisis

Abstract The golden decade of the 1970s was followed by a long-lasting stagnation that strongly affected the standards of living. Alongside a surge of violence, the structural reason behind Colombia's economic stagnation was again the excessive government interventionism in the allocation of resources. The steps toward economic liberalisation of the early 1970s ceased in 1978.

In the early 1980s, Chile and Colombia showed a similar GDP per capita. The former underwent outstanding productivity-driven growth from the mid-1980s onwards due to a set of policy reforms, while Colombia remained stagnant. Despite the fact that Colombia implemented similar reforms in the early 1990s, the benefits of such policies could not be fully achieved in that decade due to an expansionary fiscal policy from 1994 onwards, which culminated in a financial crisis in 1999.

Keywords Economic stagnation • Structural reforms • Total factors productivity • Financial crisis • Chile

In 2001, the real GDP per capita of Colombia was slightly lower than that of 1980. For most of this 20-year period, Colombia's economy showed very poor performance, which, alongside the profound financial crisis that began in 1998, moved the country to a situation of long-lasting economic stagnation of 20 years. Such long economic stagnancy had not been seen

I. Luzardo-Luna, *Colombia's Slow Economic Growth*,
Palgrave Studies in Economic History,
https://doi.org/10.1007/978-3-030-25755-2_6

since the late nineteenth century, which led to a substantial deterioration of the population's standard of living. In addition to this, the last two decades of the twentieth century were a very violent time in Colombian history, due to the violence that surged in the 1980s with the drug cartels, and between the state and guerrilla and paramilitary groups in the 1990s.

By the late 1970s, the perspectives on Colombia's future were very optimistic as the country was enjoying a period of rapid economic growth and undergoing improvements in social indicators. Such progress was, however, reversed in the early 1980s with the onset of the Latin America debt crisis in the economic area, and the surge in violence with relation to the drug cartels. Although by the middle of the 1970s, some policy-makers were focused on Colombia becoming 'the Japan of Latin America', in the 1980s, such an aspiration not only looked unfeasible, but contrasted against the reality of the stagnant economy and, for a country immersed in a spiral of violence, this dream was unlikely to become a reality any time soon.

Figure 6.1 presents the real GDP per capita for Argentina, Chile, Colombia, and Mexico. In the early 1980s, Chile and Colombia showed a

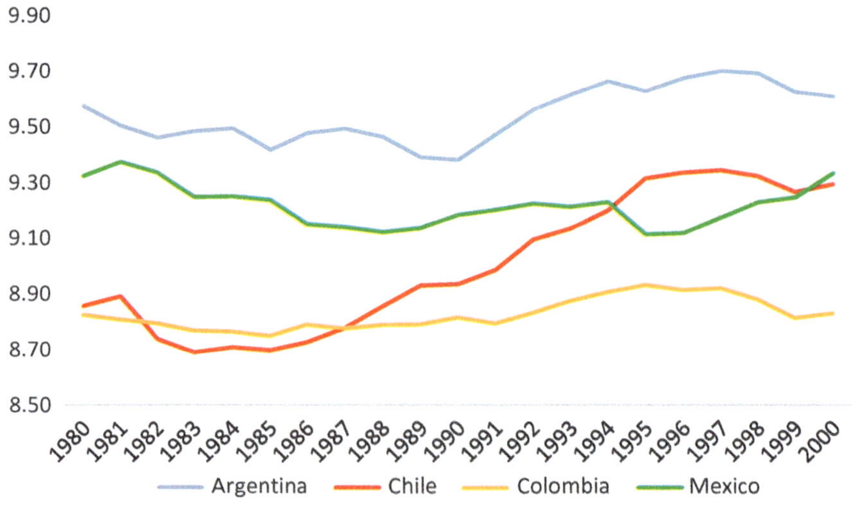

Fig. 6.1 Real GDP per capita at 2011 US$ prices (logs), 1980–2000 (Sources: Maddison Project Database, Version 2018. Bolt, Jutta, Robert Inklaar, Herman de Jong and Jan Luiten van Zanden (2018))

similar GDP per capita. The former, however, underwent outstanding economic growth from the mid-1980s, while Colombia remained stagnant. The fundamental difference between the two countries was that Chile embarked on a set of policy reforms in the 1980s, which allowed its integration into the world economy. On the other hand, Colombia waited until the 1990s to open its economy, although not with the same intensity as Chile did.

6.1 A Mild Debt Crisis, Fiscal Adjustment, and the Return of Protectionism, 1980–1990

The financial reforms of 1974 and tariff reductions of the 1970s cannot be classed as full economic liberalisation. Even if they loosened the intensity of interventionism, the government maintained high discretionary powers on credit allocation, and Colombia was still far from taking part in free trade with the largest of the world's economies. Such reforms, however, triggered a slow transition from the import-substitution model and more towards a free market economy, which was achieved in the 1990s.

In 1978, President Alfonso López Michelsen's administration concluded, and with it ceased the austerity approach towards fiscal policy. The new administration of President Julio César Turbay Ayala expanded public spending significantly to support its development plan known as the *Plan de Integración Nacional*—PIN (National Integration Plan), which established large investments in energy and communication. To fund their plans, the government expanded its external debt, taking advantage of the availability of resources in the international capital markets. After 1973, international capital markets increased their investment in developing countries, looking for higher returns. In the 1970s, several countries in Latin America entered a downward spiral of increasing debt, and this situation culminated with the debt crises of the 1980s with the so-called *lost decade*.

In 1979, Paul Volcker was appointed as the Chairman of the Federal Reserve—the FED. The new leadership of the FED had as its main priority the reduction of inflation in the United States, for which a sudden and significant increase in interest rates was necessary. They reached 20% in the early 1980s, substantially higher than the 5% observed in 1977. The new FED's policy increased debt costs for some Latin American countries, as many of the loans that had been contracted in the 1970s were made at a variable interest rate, which were automatically adjusted by the London

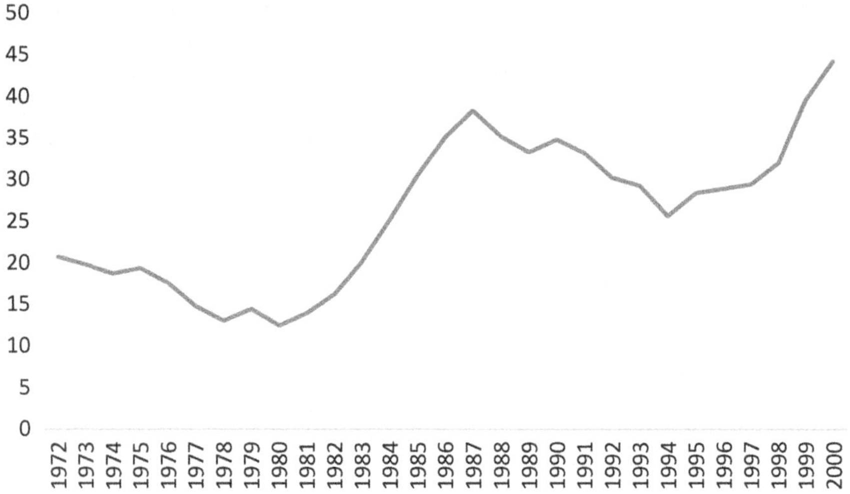

Fig. 6.2 Colombia's public debt, 1973–2000 (% of GDP) (Source: International Monetary Fund, n.d.)

Interbank Offered Rate—LIBOR (Marichal, 2014). In August 1982, the Mexican government announced that it could no longer continue to service its debt payments, and this led to general panic in the international financial markets, which stopped capital flow towards Latin America. The countries in the region found themselves in a situation of high debt costs and a lack of fresh loans, which generated a wave of defaults and calls for those debts to be restructured. In fact, Colombia was the only country in Latin America that continued servicing their debt payments throughout the whole crisis.

Colombia only joined the 'debt boom' of the 1970s in 1979, which prevented the country from reaching the level of debt observed in other countries (see Fig. 6.3), and allowed for better management of the crisis in 1982. Figure 6.2 shows Colombia's public debt as a percentage of the GDP. The low deficits of the 1970s, and the fiscal surplus between 1976 and 1978, allowed public debt to substantially reduce to 12.4% of the GDP in 1980. However, such a level, quickly increased to 16.2% in 1982.

Despite Colombia's situation not being as extreme as in the other countries, the country was profoundly affected by the 1980s debt crisis, and the government faced financial constraints which only overtook after

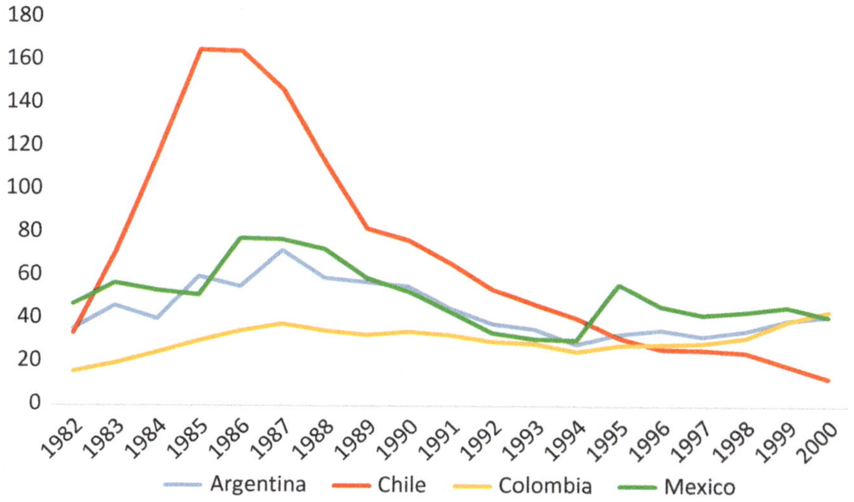

Fig. 6.3 Public debt as percentage of GDP, 1982–2000 (%) (Source: International Monetary Fund, n.d.)
Note: 1996 for Colombia is an estimated value, and is the average between 1995 and 1997

strong fiscal adjustments. Such orthodox policy allowed Colombia to maintain at least some access to foreign credit in the worse of the crisis. The actual fact is that due to Colombia's exemplary behaviour, the government had enough credibility to obtain fresh loans, and it continued to increase the public debt further from 1987 onwards (see Fig. 6.2). The effects of such a huge increase would be felt twelve years later in 1999, when Colombia experienced its worse financial crisis since the One Thousands Days War.

The increase in public debt in the early 1980s was a consequence of a shift in economic policy. After the reforms of the 1970s, the government changed its interventionism towards credit allocation that once supported various favoured sectors, such as coffee, to investing in large public-owned companies such as those in the mining and energy sectors. Table 6.1 presents the composition of public debt between 1974 and 1983. Almost 44% of public debt contracted over these years was down to public companies in the energy and mining sectors, many of which went bankrupt, or were privatised because of their accumulated losses in the 1990s. In fact, one

Table 6.1 Colombia's public debt composition, 1974–1983 (millions of constant 1975 USD)

Industry	*Company*	*Value (millions of USD, 1975 = 100)*	*Share (%)*
Energy	ISA	165	
	CORELCA	41.3	
	EEEB	140.5	
	ICEL	126.3	
	Total energy	473.1	23.3
Communications	TELECOM	7.4	
	Total communication	7.4	0.4
Mining	CARBOCOL	29.9	
	ECOPETROL	317.7	
	IFI	69	
	Total mining	416.6	20.6
Central government	Central government	1129.5	55.7
Total debt	Total debt	2026.60	100

Source: Garay (1991)

reason that the Colombian government looked to maintain its access to capital markets was to fund the ongoing investment in the pipeline and oil fields of the Caño Limón construction project (Junguito, 2018, p. 432).

Similar to the case for coffee during the import-substitution era, contracting external debt to support large public-owned companies was a mobilisation of resources towards a favoured sector and away from the rest of the economy. This time, the misallocation of resources was, however, much more significant than during the import substitution era. Due to the government's greater access to the international capital markets, it had more discretionary power in allocating capital, and indeed used this power to move resources towards public-owned companies. Despite there being less interventionism ideologically than the government of the *Frente Nacional*, the government had a lot more resources in the 1980s, and therefore greater ability to distort the markets.

Table 6.2 presents the drivers behind economic growth in the twentieth century. Between 1981 and 1996, economic growth slowed down substantially, despite there being an acceleration in investment due to the TFP being negative. Colombia's economy was accumulating capital as never before in its history. The economy's problem was no longer the lack the resources, but the misspending of such vast sums of money. The

Table 6.2 Drivers of economic growth, 1981–1996

Period	*GDP growth*	*Contribution of capital*	*Contribution of labour force*	*TFP*
1905–1929	5.75	0.71	1.13	3.92
1930–1945	3.46	0.88	1.18	1.41
1946–1958	4.74	1.82	1.07	1.84
1959–1980	5.31	1.94	1.59	1.78
1981–1996	3.71	2.173	1.90	– 0.36
1905–1996	4.74	1.40	1.43	1.90

Source: Urrutia, Pontón, and Posada (2002)

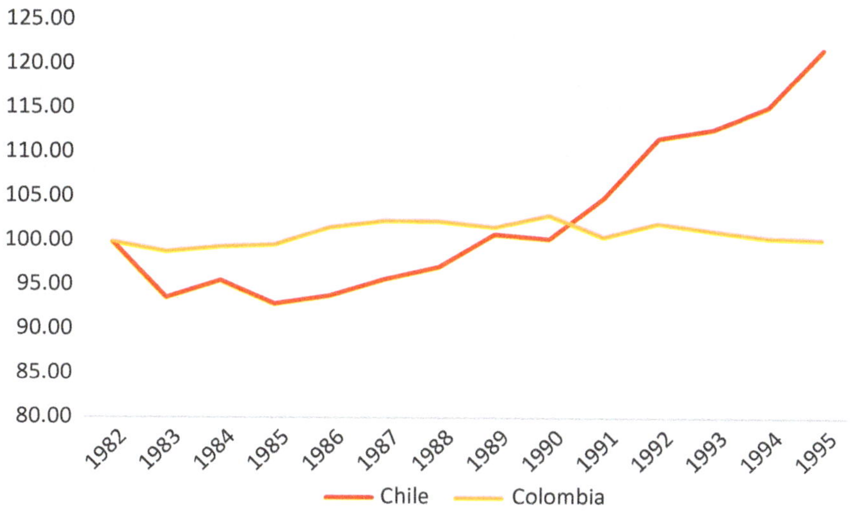

Fig. 6.4 Index of TFP, 1982–1995 (1982 = 100) (Source: Estimated based on Feenstra, Inklaar, & Timmer, 2015)

situation of the last two decades of the twentieth century was the opposite of what was seen between the period of 1905–1929, when productivity was the main driver behind economic growth, fuelled by expansion of the railways network. In other words, the misspending of the 1980s was probably more severe than the so-called *dance of the millions* in the 1920s.

The behaviour of the TFP (Fig. 6.4) was the main reason behind the divergence between Colombia and Chile's GDP per capita path in the 1980s and the early 1990s. While the latter saw an outstanding rise in

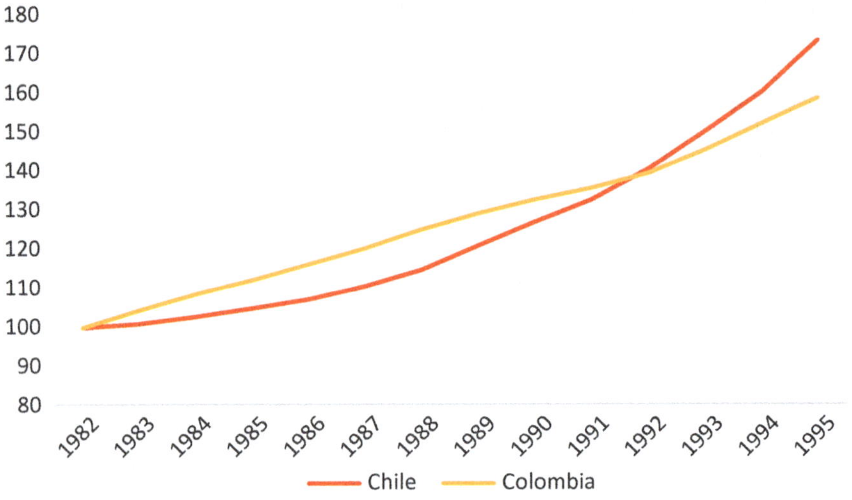

Fig. 6.5 Index of real capital accumulation, 1982–1995 (1982 = 100) (Source: Estimated based on Feenstra et al., 2015)

productivity from 1985, Colombia experienced a period of productivity stagnation in the 1980s and a mild decline in the early 1990s. The productivity trend is the difference between the so-called *Chilean Miracle,* boosted by the structural reforms of the 1980s, and Colombia's stagnation at the end of the twentieth century. Both countries showed a similar GDP per capita in 1982, and both followed a similar path in terms of capital accumulation (see Fig. 6.5), but their productivity trends diverged.

The difference in productivity growth between Chile and Colombia can be noted by observing the behaviour of exports. In 1980, the two countries also had a similar level of exports to GDP as can be observed in Fig. 6.6. The significant increase in Chile's productivity relied to a large extent on the fact that this country was able to absorb and adapt mass production technology, for example, in the food, drink, and agricultural goods industry. This allowed Chile to expand its export base, and ultimately, to propel its own economic growth. On the other hand, Colombia showed stagnation from 1986, which was related to the fact that capital allocation was distorted by the government, which had focused on the mining and energy industries through large public-owned companies.

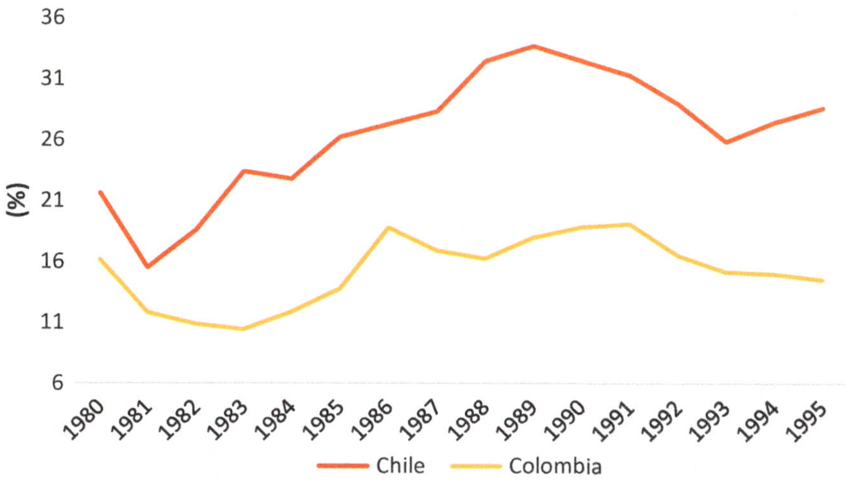

Fig. 6.6 Exports as % of the GDP, 1980–1995 (Source: World Bank, Global Development Data, n.d.)

Some of the government's investments were successful, as was the case for oil. Thanks to the access to capital markets in the 1980s, Colombia was able to build the Caño Limón fields, and pipeline. In 1986, after more than ten years, the country could start to export oil again. This time, however, oil exports reached a much higher scale than early in the twentieth century, and in 1990, the export of oil replaced coffee as Colombia's main export. Not all government investments had the same good fortune. Some public-owned companies, such as Carbocol and Corelca, showed sustained losses and were privatised and closed, respectively, in the 1990s. The misallocation of resources was so significant that it prevented any credit going to other sectors in which higher productivity could have been achieved.

In 1980, 18% of the employed population worked in the trade sector, a share that increased to 25% in 1995, when this sector overtook agriculture and became Colombia's main employment sector. At the same time, between 1980 and 1995, trade saw a huge decline in real labour productivity (see Table 6.3). In 1995, the real labour productivity of trade was only 68% of what had been reached in 1980, and this factor had a profound effect on aggregate labour productivity due to the overwhelming share that this sector had compared to the overall population of workers.

Table 6.3 Index of real labour productivity growth, 1980–1995 (1980 = 100, constant 2005 CH$ and COP$, respectively)

Sector	*Chile*	*Colombia*
Agriculture	261	122
Mining	135	202
Manufacturing	125	83
Utilities	125	145
Construction	139	73
Trade	98	68
Transport, storage, and communication	139	96
Finance, insurance, real estate, and business services	57	175
Community, social, and personal services	97	101

Source: Feenstra et al. (2015)

In the 1980s, Colombia entered into another cycle of violence as a result of the war against the drug cartels. The violence became even worse in the early 1990s, when the guerrilla and paramilitary groups increased their aggression, which again accelerated the forced migration of villagers to the cities. As during the period of *La Violencia*, many of these newcomers arriving to the cities went to work in low-productivity businesses in the trade sector. Such a flow of workers, from agriculture towards low-productivity occupations in the trade sector, was the main reason behind a stagnation in productivity and a new rise in the so-called informal economy. These two sectors were the main employers in Colombia's labour market, as they accounted for around half of all employment positions in the 1980s. In other words, the stagnation in overall productivity was a consequence of the economy mobilising workers from low-productivity sectors—agriculture—towards one where productivity was declining—trade.

An important question at this point, is why did capital not mobilise towards the trade sector? Large investments in such a sector could have increased, or at least sustained real labour productivity, as was the case for Chile, and it could have averted the overall stagnancy in productivity. Investment instead went mainly to the mining and utility sectors, where the government was the main player. In funding the large public-owned companies via external debt, the government mobilised capital towards this favoured sector, which took advantage of the benefits of having access to international capital markets. In fact, the conditions with regard to foreign loans improved in the 1980s, as can be observed in Table 6.4.

Table 6.4 Credit conditions of long and medium-term external public debt, 1982–1990

Year	*Value*	*Average interest rate (nominal)*
1982	2365	10.5
1983	1458	10.7
1984	2736	9.2
1985	2319	8.9
1986	1699	8
1987	838	8
1988	2420	7.9
1989	2874	9.2
1990	1248	8.3

Source: Garay (1991, p. 675)

On the other hand, the costs of external debt were paid for by the whole economy. As part of the adjustment policy necessary to maintain the government's credibility in the markets, and to sustain the exchange rate, Colombia increased its domestic interest rates. Figure 6.7 shows the average domestic lending interest rates for Chile and Colombia. The borrowing costs in the domestic market, which were the only sources of credit for most firms, actually became worse in the 1980s. The mismatch between the benefits of external credit, which were captured by only a few firms, and the costs, which were paid by all firms, explains the reason for the concentrated investment in the mining and utility sectors. In other words, the benefits of government access to the financial markets did not spread to the whole economy, which is what probably led to the overinvestment in the favoured sectors. That was the important difference in Chile, where structural reforms such as the banks law and the privatisations of the 1980s allowed the benefits of improvements in international credit conditions to spread to the entire economy.

The decline in labour productivity was also felt in the industrial sector, which endured a complicated period in the 1980s and reduced its share towards the GDP. In that decade, the global economy started to move to a phase of deindustrialisation, where the industrial sector reduced in size in many countries, and the sector became concentrated in only a few very competitive economies such as the Asian Tigers. In this context, Colombia as well as the rest of Latin America faced a critical decision: whether to become more competitive and develop a world-class industry, or to protect its national industry by raising tariffs and/or implementing other

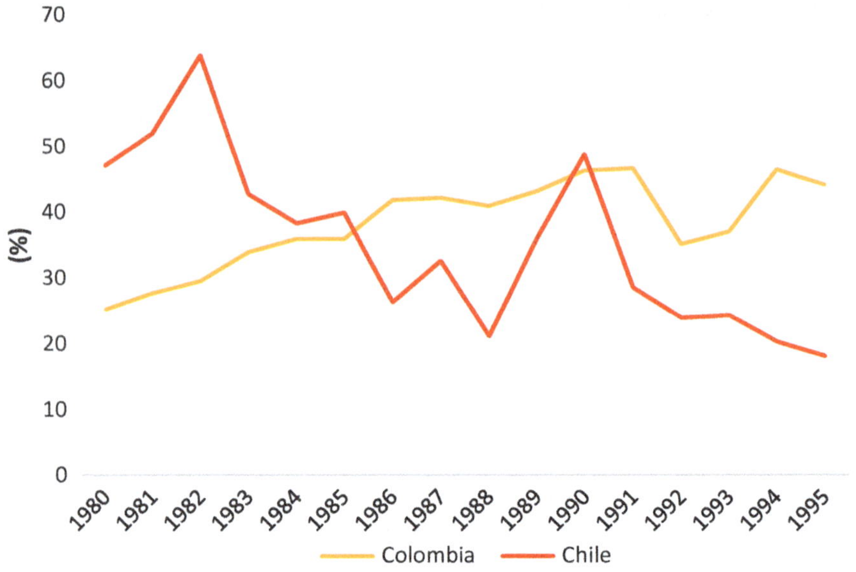

Fig. 6.7 Average lending interest rate for Chile and Colombia, 1980–1990 (%) (Source: World Bank, Global Development Data, n.d.)

trade barriers. The first option meant modernisation, technological upgrades, and, ultimately, productivity growth. The second option, which Colombia finally chose, meant returning to the protectionism mandate of the import substitution era, which led to a gradual loss of competitiveness, which eventually led to a loss of significance for the industrial sector in the following decades.

The liberalisation reforms implemented in the 1970s were reversed by President Belisario Betancur's administration (1982–1986), which heavily increased tariffs and other import restrictions (Ocampo, 2015, p. 308). Despite such restrictions being later moderated in the 1980s, they still remained relatively high by the end of the decade. Table 6.5 presents the source of demands for Colombian industry between 1945 and 1998. The increase in protectionism led to the strengthening of import substitution as the driver for industrial growth. This fact was different from that observed in the 1970s boom, when industry grew—mostly based on the domestic market, and import substitution only played a marginal role. With the return to increased protectionism, the adverse effects on input-

Table 6.5 Sources of demand of Colombian industry (%)

Source	*1945–1965*	*1970–1979*	*1981–1987*	*1987–1998*
Import substitution	40	6.2	23.2	−95.8
Domestic demand	56	85.5	65.1	159.7
External demand	3	8.3	11.7	36.1

Source: Echavarria and Villamizar (2007)

Table 6.6 Source of funding (%)

Period	*Retained earnings*	*Capital contribution*	*Loans*	*Total*
1970–1974	46.8	6.5	46.7	100
1976–1978	36.6	4.8	58.6	100
1981–1985	44.6	4.9	50.5	100
1986–1999	50.7	5.2	44.1	100

Source: Echavarria and Villamizar (2007)

importation returned, and this contributed to the slow growth in industrial productivity. Echavarria and Villamizar (2007) find a positive relationship between importation and industrial performance for Colombia in the twentieth century, pointing out the importance of the availability of affordable inputs for industrial development.

Besides protectionism, the industrial sector also suffered from high borrowing costs, which again aggravated the chronic problem with regard to the lack of financial leverage. Table 6.6 shows the source of funding for the industrial sector between 1970 and 1999. In the 1980s, loans reduced their share as a source of funding, which made industrial firms highly dependent on retained earnings as a means of financing their investments. Again, the lack of a strong banking system was a major constraint in Colombia's industrial development.

6.2 The Economic Liberalisation, 1990–1994

In the late 1980s, the flaws of protectionism were notorious, and it was ever more the consensus among policy-makers, the necessity for integrating Colombia into the world economy. The trigger for economic liberalisation, however, came in July 1989 when the International Coffee Agreement came to an end, leaving the international coffee prices and the quantity exported, ruled by the market forces. The new situation reinforced the thesis that Colombia should improve its competitiveness by giving more power to the private sector, and that it must reduce its government's interventionism. Such views were in line with the so-called Washington consensus, which became the mainstream mindset among Colombian economists.

The first step towards economic liberalisation finally came in March 1990, during the final year of the President Virgilio Barco's administration (1986–1990), although the measures were very moderate. The actual reforms with regard to liberalisation were implemented during President Cesar Gaviria's administration (1990–1994), which was aware of the necessity for a new development framework based on exports, and the opening up of the economy to foreign investors. This required an ambitious set of structural reforms, which changed Colombia's economy and propelled its economic growth in the early twenty-first century.

The most famous of the Gaviria's reforms was the *Apertura Económica* (Economic Opening), which consisted of a substantial reduction in tariffs and other constraints to international trade. According to Edwards and Steiner (2008), the nominal rate of protection, which includes tariffs and imports surcharges, was reduced to 11.8% in February 1992, from 41.6% in 1989. For the first time since the Great Depression of 1929, importing was accessible for most firms, which facilitated the supply of inputs and capital goods. The main beneficiaries of the *Apertura Económica* were, however, not firms but consumers, who suddenly had access to a more diverse range, and higher quality goods. During the protectionist era, smuggling and black markets were very common in Colombia. All major cities had shopping areas known as *San Andresitos*, where electronics, appliances, drinks, or confectionary (usually from smuggling sources) were sold at lower prices than in legal trading. Smuggling was probably another reason for the underinvestment in trade, and hence its decline in productivity between 1980 and 1995.

The second major structural reform was the elimination of capital controls with Law 9 of 1991. This reform, strongly endorsed by the Ministry of Finance's Rudolf Hommes, looked for facilitation of capital flow, and a higher degree of flexibility in the management of exchange rates. This was a precondition for another government aim—an independent Central Bank, with inflation control as its main task.

All of the reform packages were a transition from dirigisme, an economy where the state guides or manages the economy and actively intervenes in the market, towards a more regulatory role of government. The new paradigm allowed substantial transformations, such as the participation of private firms in the utilities, healthcare, and pension sectors. They remained heavily regulated by the government, but the public policy action moved from supply-side subsidies (via public-owned utilities firms or hospitals) to demand-side subsidies. The latter has predominated ever since then, and consists of private enterprises offering services such as electricity or healthcare, and the government partially or completely covering the fees for those in the low-income population.

The increased role of private firms in the provision of public services did not mean cuts in social expenditure. The main reform under Gaviria's administration was a new constitution, which came into force in 1991. The new *Carta Magna* established a set of social security services, such as health, pension, and education, which were guaranteed by the government. Likewise, Colombia moved towards a decentralised state, where local governments assumed more responsibility, but also demanded more resources from the central government. The new government's financial commitments led to a gradual increase in public expenditure over the following years, which ended in structural fiscal deficit, despite the successive tax increases.

The liberalisation reforms of the early 1990s have shaped Colombia's economy up until now. The following governments, especially after 1998, continued to expand on the liberal model with policies such as free trade agreements, or permitting oil extraction by foreign companies in the 2000s. Despite economic liberalisation setting the groundwork for strong economic growth between 2001 and 2015, they probably came very late in fully taking advantage of the globalisation wave that the world economy saw in the 1990s. This global integration allowed vast amounts of foreign investment to be directed to regions such as East Asia, or countries such as Chile, but it also increased the potential risk for financial crises spreading, which actually did occur in 1998.

6.3 The Social Leap, Fiscal Deficit, and Financial Crisis, 1994–2000

In 1994, the new administration of President Ernesto Samper Pizano (1994–1998) came into power. His administration did not fully share the free market approach of the former government. The new administration looked for an economic model that was different from both the protectionism of the import-substitution era and the liberalism of the early 1990s (Junguito, 2018). The Samper's development plan, called *el Salto Social* (the Social Leap) was something similar to a welfare state, which combined free markets with high public expenditure on social assistance.

Based on optimistic estimations of economic growth (Junguito, 2018), the government increased public expenditure, which reached 17%[1] of the GDP in 1998 from 12.8% at the beginning of the administration in 1994. As the government's revenues did not grow at the same pace, there was a significant increase in the fiscal deficit, and this ultimately led to the accumulation of public debt (see Fig. 6.2). The combination of high external debt, fiscal deficit, and a stronger integration into the world economy, initiated by the opening up of the economy, left Colombia in a vulnerable situation with regard to any negative shock in the international capital markets.

Financial turbulence arrived in July 1997 when the Asian financial crisis began. The initial effect of the crisis on Colombia, however, was mild. Table 6.7 presents the credit rating of Colombia, and its government bond spread. In the case of the latter, the indicator presented is the EMBI+[2] global composite estimated by J.P. Morgan, which compares Colombia's bond yield regarding a weighted average of developing countries' spread. In other words, the EMBI+ allows one to see how risky Colombian bonds were perceived in relation to the average of those in other emerging markets.

The Asian crisis heightened the investors' aversion to lending to developing countries, which were by now perceived as riskier. The rise of global uncertainty reduced the flow of capital to developing countries, and therefore to Colombia, which at that time was accumulating substantial fiscal deficit. Because of this situation, in October 1997, Standard & Poor's revised Colombia's credit rating, down from positive, to stable. That had a negative effect on the country's borrowing costs, as the EMBI+ spread reached a closing level of 200 basis points the same month, before increasing to 283 basis points in November 1997.

The greatest impact came on 17 August 1998, when the financial crisis propagated to Russia, where this country reacted with strong devaluation, and defaulted on its external debts (Kaminsky & Reinhart, 2001). The

[1] Source: Junguito and Rincon (2004).

[2] EMBI are estimated on Brandy bonds, while EMBI+ also includes Eurobonds.

Table 6.7 Credit rating history of Colombia and EMBI+ Colombia government bond spread, February 1997–September 1999

Month	*Feb-97*	*Jul-97*	*Oct-97*	*Sep-98*	*Jun-99*	*Sep-99*
Credit rating Standard & Poor's (long-term foreign currency ratings)	BBB−/positive	BBB−/positive	BBB−/stable	BBB−/stable	BBB−/negative	BB+/stable
EMBI+ Colombia government bond spread (basic points)	149	147	200	1090	667	613

Source: For Credit rating Rowland (2004), and Kaminsky and Reinhart (2001) For September 1998
Note: For EMBI+ Bond Spread: Global Financial Data Finaeon (n.d.)

Russian default moved the situation to another level, and what was initially an Asian financial crisis, became a global financial crisis. The impact was heavy on Latin America, and countries such as Argentina and Venezuela reached a bond spread[3] peak on 27 August with levels of 1525 and 4098 basis points, respectively (Kaminsky & Reinhart, 2001). Colombia saw its spread peak on 15 September with 1090 (Kaminsky & Reinhart, 2001), although it declined quickly after some weeks (Rowland, 2004).

The crisis arrived in Colombia at the beginning of a new administration led by President Andrés Pastrana Arango (1998–2002). The president's administration spent some time before it reacted to the crisis. The government took some fiscal measures in late 1998, and established a Tobin tax, known as '2 × 1000', a levy of two Colombian pesos for every 1000 was imposed on financial transactions. The most important measure, however, was implemented the following year when the economic situation deteriorated even further.

By early 1999, Colombia was immersed in a systemic crisis. The country was experiencing a financial crisis, an exchange rate crisis, a fiscal crisis, high unemployment, and violence due to armed conflicts between the state and irregular groups all being at their height, and all at the same time (Junguito, 2018). The options for crisis management were less than those available in 1982, when the country favoured the orthodox fiscal policy during López Michelsen's administration (1975–1978).

The crisis worsened in September 1999 when Colombia lost its investment grade from Standard and Poor's, as the agency downgraded the country's rating from BBB– to BB+ (see Table 6.5). The situation had the potential to worsen the crisis, which could have ended in debt default, which had occurred in Argentina. Under these circumstances, Colombia's government looked for an agreement with the International Monetary Fund (IMF) to obtain fresh loans known as the *External Fund Facility*. As part of the agreement, which included the monitoring of macroeconomic management, Colombia committed to making substantial fiscal adjustments, restructuring its banking system and other structural reforms. Before signing the agreement, Colombia changed its exchange rate policy from a band system[4] towards a free-floating framework. The decision to do this was strongly influenced by the Department of Treasury in the

[3] This spread is relative to the US treasury bond.

[4] This system, also known as Sliding Exchange-rate Band System, allows the exchange rate fluctuation, but within a certain rate determined by the central bank.

United States, whose endorsement was essential for the IMF's support (Junguito, 2018).

The agreement was finally approved by the IMF's directorate on 20 December 1999, and Colombia was given access to US$ 2.7 billion (Junguito, 2018). The agreement was followed by a set of structural reforms such as the Legislative Act 01 of 2000, which reduced the transfers from the Central Government to local administrations, in order to balance the budget. Likewise, the government obtained resources from privatisation, which commenced in the early 1990s as part of the economy's liberalisation. Despite the government's efforts, the crisis from 1999 meant a decline in GDP of 4.2%, a drop even greater than that seen in 1931, the gravest period of the Great Depression. The reforms of 1999 contributed to overcoming the crisis, but could also be seen as a second generation of liberalisation policies, which created the conditions for the fast economic growth experienced in the early twenty-first century.

In spite of government structural reforms, and the IMF's support, Colombia's recovery was slow. In 2000 and 2001, the GDP grew by just 2.9% and 1.4%, respectively. An important reason behind the slow economic recovery was the intensification of armed confrontations between the state and insurgent groups, especially the Revolutionary Armed Forces of Colombia—FARC which was the largest guerrilla unit (Kalmanovitz, 2017). The FARC increased their terrorist actions, and crimes between the late 1990s and early 2000s, which moved the country into generalised chaos. This situation strongly affected Colombia's stability, economic investment, and its perception from the international capital markets point of view.

Figure 6.8 shows Colombia's bond spread between May 1999 and October 2001. Despite Colombia implementing the most important structural reforms in 1999, the country's debt spread not only remained high, but it worsened in 2000. In fact, it was only after 2002 that Colombia began to see significant improvements in security, and economic recovery actually took place.

The deep financial crisis had painful consequences on the population's standards of living. According to the World Bank, in 1992, 47% of Colombia's population were living below the poverty line, established in $5.5 (2011 dollars, PPP). This rate reached 60.5% by 2011, which indicates the intensity of the crisis. The force behind the increasing poverty levels was probably the huge deterioration of the labour market. By 1999, the rate of unemployment was 20.1% (see Fig. 6.9), significantly higher than the 8.3% observed in 1994.

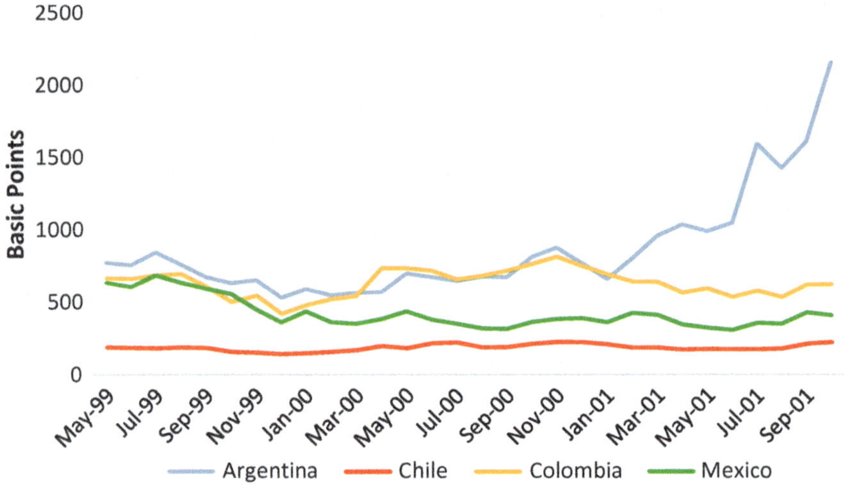

Fig. 6.8 EMBI+ government bond spread (closing monthly values, basic points) (Source: Global Financial Data Finaeon, n.d.)

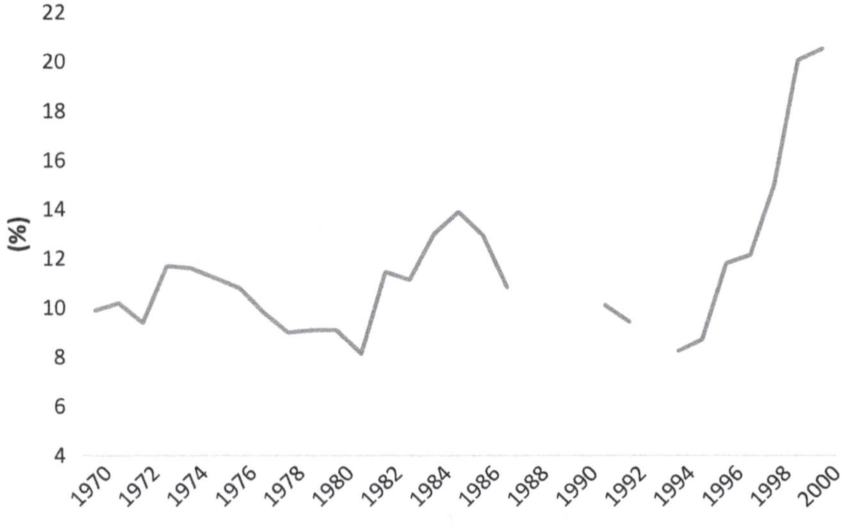

Fig. 6.9 Unemployment rate, 1970–2000 (%) (Source: For 1970–1979: Londoño (1995); For 1980–2000: World Bank, Global Development Data (n.d.))

The last two decades of the twentieth century were certainly a traumatic period in Colombia's history. In addition to the terrible violence, the country endured a long-lasting period of economic stagnation, which impeded a more rapid improvement in standards of living. Despite the promising perspectives concerning the industrial sector in the 1970s, the high level of government interventionism in resource allocation in the 1980s prevented the industrial sector from receiving the financial resources it needed for modernisation. Unable to increase its competitiveness, Colombia embarked on a path towards deindustrialisation, which closed the door to achieving development through mass production technology. Likewise, the benefits of the economic liberalisation in the early 1990s could not be achieved in the same decade due to Colombia moving towards an unorthodox fiscal policy from 1994 onwards. This fact meant the accumulation of substantial fiscal deficits and external debt, and finally culminated in the worst economic crisis for the country since the Great Depression.

References

Echavarria, J., & Villamizar, M. (2007). El proceso Colombiano de desindustrialización. In M. Urrutia & J. Robinson (Eds.), *Economía colombiana del siglo XX: un análisis cuantitativo*. Bogota: Fondo de Cultura Económica.

Edwards, S., & Steiner, R. (2008). *La revolución incompleta: las reformas de Gaviria*. Bogota: Grupo editorial Norma y Fedesarrollo.

Feenstra, R., Inklaar, R., & Timmer, M. (2015). The Next Generation of the Penn World Table. *American Economic Review, 105*(10), 3150–3182. Retrieved from https://www.rug.nl/ggdc/productivity/pwt/

Garay, L. (1991). *Colombia y la crisis de la deuda*. Bogota: CINEP and Universidad Nacional.

Global Financial Data Finaeon. (n.d.). *Global Financial Data Database and Indices*. Retrieved from http://www.globalfinancialdata.com/

International Monetary Fund. (n.d.). *A Historical Public Debt Database* (2010). Abbas, A., Belhocine, N., ElGanainy, A., and Horton, M. WP/10/245. Retrieved from https://www.imf.org/external/datamapper/datasets/DEBT

Junguito, R. (2018). *Cien Episodios de la Historia Económica de Colombia*. Bogota: Ariel.

Junguito, R., & Rincon, H. (2004). La Politica Fiscal en el siglo XX en Colombia. In M. Urrutia & E. Posada (Eds.), *Investigaciones recientes sobre historia económica colombiana*. Banco de la República Reportes del Emisor, No. 62.

Kalmanovitz, S. (2017). *Nueva Historia Económica de Colombia*. Bogota: Universidad Jorge Tadeo Lozano.

Kaminsky, G., & Reinhart, C. (2001). *Financial Markets in Times of Stress*. NBER Working Paper Series.

Londoño, J. (1995). *Distribución del Ingreso y Desarrollo Económico: Colombia en el siglo XX*. Bogota: Tercer Milenio.

Maddison Project Database, Version 2018. Bolt, Jutta, Robert Inklaar, Herman de Jong and Jan Luiten van Zanden. (2018). *Rebasing 'Maddison': New Income Comparisons and the Shape of Long-Run Economic Development*. Retrieved from https://www.rug.nl/ggdc/historicaldevelopment/maddison/releases/maddison-project-database-2018

Marichal, C. (2014). *Historia mínima de la deuda externa de Latinoamérica, 1820–2010*. Mexico D.F.: El Colegio de México.

Ocampo, J. (2015). *Historia Económica de Colombia*. Bogota: Fondo de Cultura Económica.

Rowland, P. (2004). *Determinants of Spread, Credit Ratings and Creditworthiness for Emerging Market Sovereign Debt: A Follow-Up Study Using Pooled Data Analysis*. Working Paper No. 296. Banco de la República, Bogota.

Urrutia, M., Pontón, A., & Posada, C. (2002). *El Crecimiento Económico Colombiano En El Siglo XX*. Bogotá: Fondo de Cultura Económica.

World Bank, Global Development Data. (n.d.). Retrieved from https://data.worldbank.org/

CHAPTER 7

Commodities-Driven Growth, 2001–2018: The Colombian Miracle

Abstract Between 2002 and 2015, Colombia entered into a stage of accelerated economic growth. The driver behind such economic expansion was the improvement in security, which paved the way for investment. The high growth rates for that period were caused by an increase in the input factors rather than by the productivity. In fact, productivity has consistently declined throughout the twenty-first century, which is associated with the informal economy.

The high proportion of informal companies observed in Colombia is a result of the heavy tax burden, which means to take part in the formal economy. Firms' maturity process is significantly affected in a way that they remain small, and without access to financial services, which prevents them from fully exploiting the possibilities that ICTs offer.

Keywords Security • Commodities • ICT • Small business • Informal economy • Chile

At the beginning of the twenty-first century, Colombia was still suffering from the 1999 crisis. In 2001, the real GDP per capita was slightly lower than that of 1980, unemployment was over 15%, and the level of poverty, measured on a line of $5.5 (2011 PPP), was over 50% of the population.

I. Luzardo-Luna, *Colombia's Slow Economic Growth*,
Palgrave Studies in Economic History,
https://doi.org/10.1007/978-3-030-25755-2_7

Besides its adverse economic performance, Colombia was suffering a bloody and violent wave as a consequence of terrorist actions of the insurgent groups.

Despite such a terrible beginning to the century, from 2002, Colombia entered into a stage of accelerated economic growth that had not been seen since the 1920s. Figure 7.1 shows the real GDP per capita in logarithms for Argentina, Chile, Colombia, and Mexico between 2000 and 2016. The driver behind such economic expansion was the improvement in security from the early 2000s onwards, which paved the way for outstanding growth in foreign and domestic investment. Colombia's advances were consolidated with the onset of peace between the government and FARC in 2016, which inaugurated an era of stability with great potential for sustained progress in the twenty-first century.

Along with the increase in investment, the strong economic growth in the early twenty-first century was strongly propelled by a super boom in commodities prices in international markets. In the case of Colombia, the consolidation of its oil industry generated a vast amount of resources, which allowed the funding of significant public expenditure. As well as in

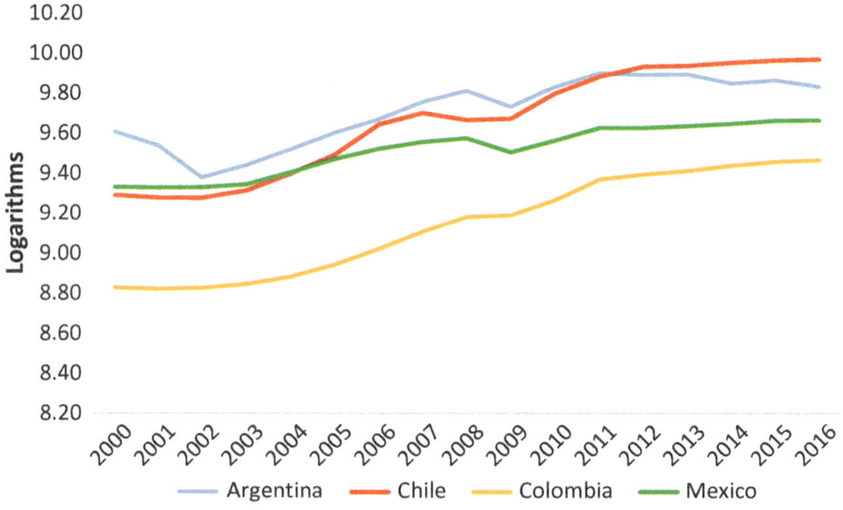

Fig. 7.1 Real GDP per capita at 2011 US$ prices (logs), 2000–2016 (logarithms, 2011 = 100) (Sources: Maddison Project Database, Version 2018. Bolt, Jutta, Robert Inklaar, Herman de Jong and Jan Luiten van Zanden (2018))

the second half of the 1990s, the first decade of this century, the Colombian government has seen a massive increase in their expenses, which is partly due to revenue from oil, but also from higher taxes. Since 1980, Colombia has implemented 13 tax reforms, most of them aimed at increasing tax rates or the number of taxpayers, which generated a heavy tax burden that affected the country's competitiveness and new emerging firms. When oil prices dropped and therefore the revenue received from that industry declined in 2014, the flaws in Colombia's economy became apparent. From 2016, Colombia entered into a new cycle of slow economic growth, which also slowed down any outstanding improvements in the standards of living.

On the other of hand, unlike for most of the twentieth century, mass production is no more the enabling general purpose technology that is boosting economic growth in the twenty-first century. This role is now filled by ICTs, which have enabled a marked increase in productivity around the world ever since the 1990s. Colombia has also incorporated ICTs into its production capacity, although its economic growth has been based on input factors (capital and labour), as productivity has seen a consistent decline in the 2000s. The large informal sector is one of the main reasons behind the decline in productivity, as this sector negatively affected firms' evolution from small to medium, and then large-sized enterprises, which is when they are able to quickly incorporate technological changes.

7.1 Improvements in Security and Investment Acceleration, 2001–2015

The structural reforms from the 1990s set the stage for Colombia's integration into the world economy, and a higher rate of economic growth. However, the lack of security initiated by terrorist actions of insurgent groups, and the financial crisis in 1999, impeded the materialisation of the structural reforms' potential. In the early 2000s, these conditions changed as security notably improved.

In 2002, President Álvaro Uribe Vélez's administration came into power (2002–2010). This administration's top policy was known as *Democratic Security*. The new government substantially increased military expenditure and improved the efficiency of the armed forces, and this reported positive results. After several military successes, the Colombian government placed the insurgent groups in remote areas of the countryside, which entailed a huge reduction in violence. The criminal homicide rate

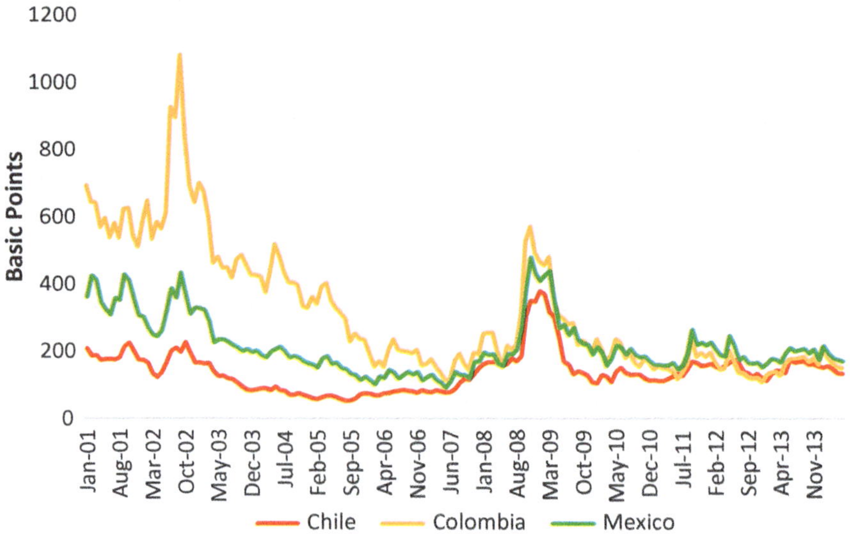

Fig. 7.2 Spread government bonds EBMI+*, January 2001 and May 2014 (basic points) (Source: Global Financial Data Finaeon, n.d.)

per 100,000 saw a substantial decline from 68.2 in 2002 to 33.6 in 2010, and kidnappings and other crimes also experienced a similar decline.

Improvements in security increased the market's confidence, which meant that investment took off, including that for foreign capital. Figure 7.2 presents the bond spread of Chile, Colombia, and Mexico between January 2001 and May 2014. In the early 2000s, Colombia was certainly perceived as more of a risky country to invest in by the capital markets than their Latin American peers. The news reported in international media was mainly related to violence and drug trafficking, and this made it very difficult to attract foreign investment, even despite the economic liberalisation of the 1990s. This situation changed throughout the 2000s, and by 2008, Colombia's spread converged with that of Chile and Mexico. In 2011, after twelve years, Colombia recovered its investment grade, which allowed it to reduce its borrowing costs and attract foreign investment.

Table 7.1 breaks down economic growth by its main drivers, but unlike the similar tables shown in the former chapters, two new variables are incorporated: the quality of labour, and ICT capital. Due to the lack of

Table 7.1 Drivers of economic growth, average 2000–2015 (%)

Variable	*Argentina*	*Chile*	*Colombia*	*Mexico*
GDP growth	2.50	4.10	4.09	2.11
Labour				
Labour quantity contribution	0.35	0.83	1.53	0.91
Labour quality contribution	0.35	0.42	0.69	0.17
Capital				
ICT capital contribution	0.24	0.68	0.51	0.28
Non-ICT capital contribution	1.32	3.17	2.68	1.00
Total factor productivity	0.24	−0.99	−1.33	−0.24

Source: The Conference Board (n.d.)

data, the quality of labour, which was essentially obtained through improvements in education, was not presented in the drivers for economic growth for the twentieth century, and its effect is included within the TFP. On the other hand, ICT capital was included in the total capital.

The high growth rates for the period of 2000–2015 were caused by an increase in the input factors rather than by the productivity factor. Capital formation was the main driver behind economic growth between 2000 and 2015, which was due to improvements in the environment for investment. Along with the rest of Latin America, Colombia strongly benefited from the commodities boom of the 2000s, propelled by the fast economic growth of Asian economies. Such outstanding expansion increased global commodities prices, and countries such as Colombia, with a large endowment of natural resources, became attractive places for investment. The oil industry reached a share of 6.8% of the GDP in 2011, more than double that of the 3.3% in 2001, becoming the driver behind economic expansion. This was the result of huge growth in oil exports, which generated the resources for funding social policies aimed at the low-income sector of the population.

Likewise, the contribution of labour quality was substantial. This fact is explained by the recovery in employment after the crisis in 1999, and the labour reforms implemented in 2002, which increased the flexibility of the labour market. Unemployment dropped from 20.5% in 2000 to 11.9% in 2005, and further to 8.3% in 2015, which allowed the incorporation of thousands of workers into the economy's production capacity. Similarly, the contribution of higher quality labour was also significant, as it was the highest between the analysed countries. This major contribution was

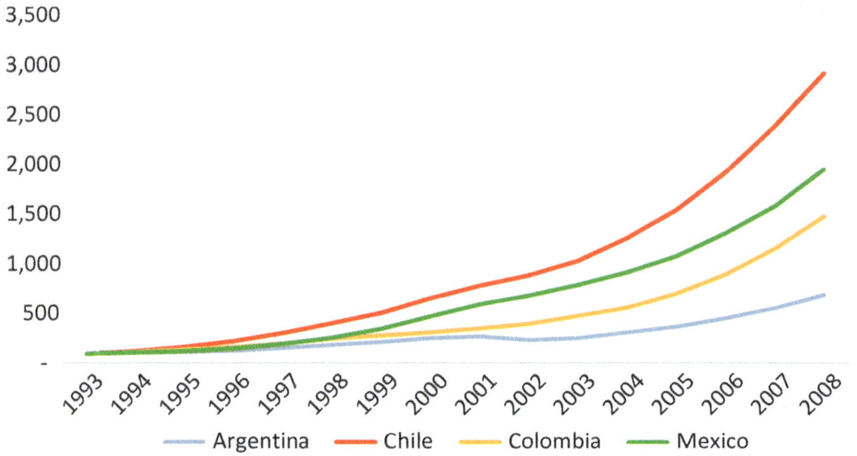

Fig. 7.3 Index of ICT capital growth, 1993–2008 (1993 = 100) (Source: Estimated based on the Conference Board, n.d.)

essentially due to improvements in schooling in the late twentieth century, but especially from the 1990s onwards.

ICT capital also notably contributed to economic growth, and on average increased the real GDP by 0.5% per annum. The ICT sector witnessed massive growth with the growth of the Internet in the 2000s, and the arrival of international companies that brought not only capital, but also know-how to the country. The contribution of ICT, however, could have been greater as the country only properly joined this new technological wave in the 2000s rather than in the 1990s, as was the case for Chile.

Figure 7.3 shows an index of ICT capital growth between 1993 and 2008. Unlike Chile and Mexico, which built significant ICT capital stocks in the late 1990s, Colombia only underwent similar expansion in the 2000s. That explains the higher contribution of ICT to economic growth between 2000 and 2015, in the sense that throughout this period, Colombia was incorporating the benefits that Chile and Mexico reached in the last few years of the twentieth century. As was the case for steam and mass production, Colombia joined, or took advantage of, the ICT revolution late, and despite rapid expansion after 2004, it could not converge with other countries in Latin America in terms of ICT stock (see Fig. 7.4). This fact had certainly a negative impact on the productivity, which showed the strongest declined among the analysed countries.

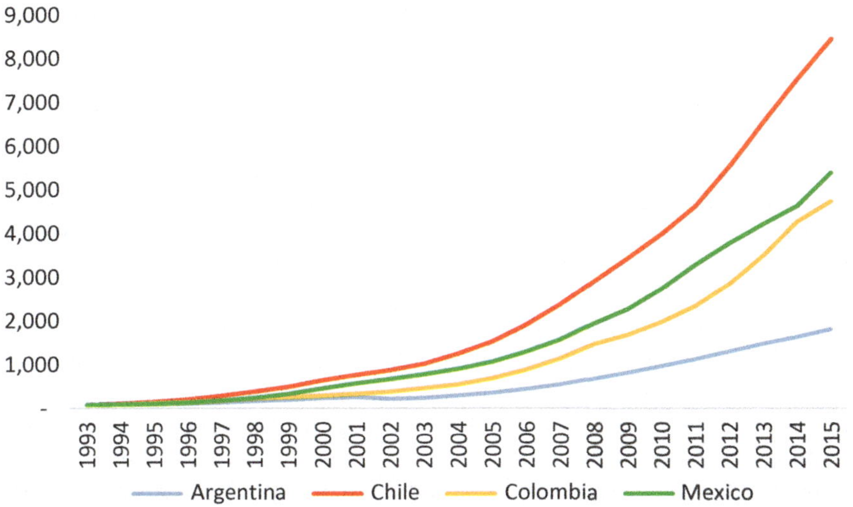

Fig. 7.4 Index of ICT capital growth, 1993–2015 (1993 = 100) (Source: Estimated based on the Conference Board, n.d.)

As in the 1990s, the productivity decline is strongly associated with the large share of the informal economy, which is particularly important in the trade sector, the main employer in Colombia from 1997. The slow incorporation of ICT technologies in trade led to a substantial share of businesses remaining operating without the possibilities that this general purpose technology offered. In 2015, the added value of an American worker in the trade sector was equivalent to 5.6[1] Colombian workers in the same sector. The gap was lower (3.3) in social and personal services, the second largest employer in Colombia, which included industries such as education and healthcare that had a higher prevalence of skilled workers. Certainly, the absorption of ICT technology was uneven in Colombia, and the backwardness of productivity in trade is related to the large share of small business operating in the informal economy which were not able to incorporate ICT technology into their operation in areas such as the distribution channels. Eslava, Garcia, Hurtado, and Pinzon (2017) find that the productivity gap between Colombia and the United States in manufacturers was mainly due to the gap between small size firms, which

[1] Source: National Productivity Council, p. 19.

were more prevalent in Colombia. There was still a productivity gap between large firms, but it was substantially smaller.

The improvements in security achieved by the Uribe's period were maintained under the administration of President Juan Manuel Santos (2010–2018), which gained landslide military successes over FARC. Once this organisation was weak and their troops reduced, President Santos established negotiations in 2012, which concluded in a peace agreement in 2016. This deal drew to a close a bloody era in Colombia's history, which allowed the consolidation of social and economic stability.

Despite productivity problems, Colombia's fast economic growth between 2002 and 2015 allowed it to not only almost double its income per capita, but also enabled outstanding social progress. Income poverty declined to 28% in 2015, from more than 50% in 2002. This fact consolidated the middle classes, which now accounts for the majority of the population in Colombia. This was a significant accomplishment, and strengthened the consumer base and human capital for sustained economic growth in the twenty-first century.

7.2 Post-Conflict and Economic Slowdown, 2016–2018

In the 2010s, Colombia moved to another plateau in its commercial integration into the world economy by signing free trade agreements with its main commercial partners. The free trade agreements with the United States came into effect in 2012, which were followed by similar agreements with the European Union in 2014, and South Korea in 2016. Likewise, in 2016, Colombia, together with Chile, Mexico, and Peru, established the Pacific Alliance, which constituted the second generation of economic integration, and went beyond standard free trade agreements.

Despite the good economic perspectives, the economy entered into a slow economic phase in 2015 as the commodities boom ended. Asian economies started to grow at more moderate rates, and the United States increased its oil production capacity, which reduced international oil prices. Oil had been consolidated as Colombia's main export, and was essential for the government's finances, which is why its price declined in late 2014, which had a negative impact on the entire economy. From an average growth rate of 4.1% between 2000 and 2015, the economy grew by only 1.9%, and 1.8% in 2016 and 2017, respectively. In 2016, when

Colombia's economic outlook looked better than ever, the flaws of economic growth based on inputs, and not on productivity, became evident.

In 2016 and 2017, the TFPs were −2.4 and −2.2, respectively. If the TFPs had been 0, the economy would have more than doubled in size. As has been the case since 1980, Colombia's economic growth problem was not due to its input factors (capital and labour), but the efficiency in the way they were used (Table 7.2).

The reasons behind the productivity decline are essentially the same as those of the commodities-boom period: a high concentration of the labour force in low-productivity sectors and firms. Both are related to a high share of small-sized businesses in trade and operating in the informal economy. Such kind of operations had significant costs, as those businesses usually did not have access to financial services, which made it more difficult to make the required investments and absorb the ICT technologies.

If small firms' sizes in trade look to be the main reason behind low productivity, it raises the questions: ***what prevented such businesses from growing and becoming medium-sized firms? What made some firms profitable operating in the informal economy, but not in the formal economy?***

The actual fact is that many small firms could not afford the costs associated with being part of the formal economy. The tax burden and other regulations were so costly that only medium- and large-sized companies could actually cover such costs. Figure 7.5 presents the total tax and contributions paid out for a medium-sized company as a percentage of its profits. The tax burdens faced by Colombian companies are substantially higher than those of Chile and Mexico, even if taking the tax reduction implemented in 2014 into account which substantially reduced employment taxes. When in 2018, the tax burden for a Chilean firm accounted for 34% of their profits, a similar Colombian company had to

Table 7.2 Drivers of economic growth, average 2016–2017 (%)

Variable	*2016*	*2017*
GDP growth	1.94	1.77
Labour quantity contribution	0.19	0.59
Labour quality contribution	0.93	0.56
ICT capital contribution	0.24	0.29
Non-ICT capital contribution	2.94	2.55
Total factor productivity	−2.36	−2.22

Source: The Conference Board (n.d.)

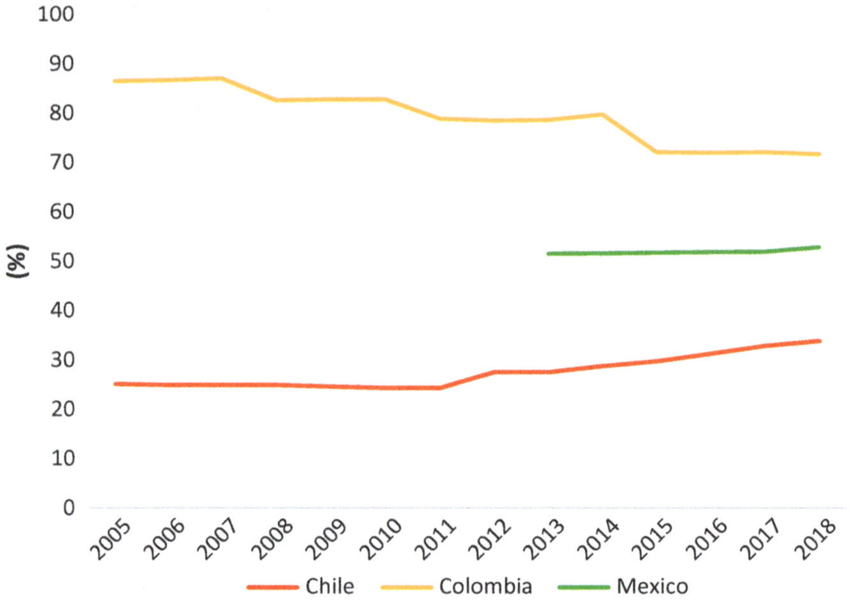

Fig. 7.5 Total tax and contribution rate, 2005–2018 (% of profit) (Source: World Bank, Global Development Data, n.d.)

pay 71.9%. Naturally, such rates only applied to firms in the formal sector, which made it very costly to make the jump from a small informal business to a medium-sized formal enterprise. The high proportion of informal companies observed in Colombia is a result of the heavy tax burden, which creates a great incentive to operate in this manner in order to avoid the tax costs that come from operating in the formal sector. In doing so, firms' maturity process is significantly affected in a way that they remain operating in the informal economy, where they cannot fully exploit the possibilities that ICTs offer. Likewise, the high tax rate explains why investment was concentrated in the oil and mining sectors during the commodities boom period (2001–2010). Only very profitable businesses could afford such a high tax burden.

One of the many problems associated with informality is that businesses in this segment do not 'take part' in the financial market. The only financial alternative for this kind of firm is informal credit, where interest rates are substantially higher than in the formal banking system. The high tax

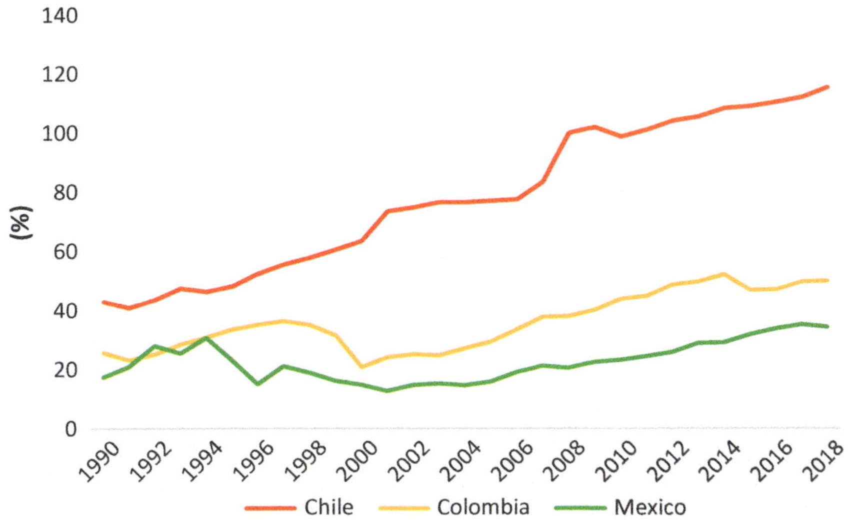

Fig. 7.6 Domestic credit to private sector, 1990–2018 (% of GDP) (Source: World Bank, Global Development Data, n.d.)

burden in Colombia is to a certain extent a barrier for small companies taking part in the financial system, and the company could instead fund its own expansion or technological upgrade. That has a negative effect on the market's structure, as the lack of competence reduces the pressure on medium- and large-sized firms with regard to innovation. The lack of credit certainly remained as a major constraint for Colombia's economy. Figure 7.6 presents domestic credit compared to the private sector as a percentage of GDP between 1990 and 2018 for Chile, Colombia, and Mexico. In the 1990s, there was already a disparity between Chile and Colombia, which increased with the 1999 crisis and has continued throughout the twenty-first century. As in the mass production era, Colombian firms lack a banking system that leverages its growth. Financial repression is no longer a constraint for the development of banking, but informality has emerged as a significant cause of friction between firms and the financial sector.

At this point it raises the question: why are Colombian taxes so high compared to other Latin America countries? The answer to this led to the substantial increase in size that the Colombian government saw from the mid-1990s (see Fig. 7.7). After 1994, public expenditure significantly

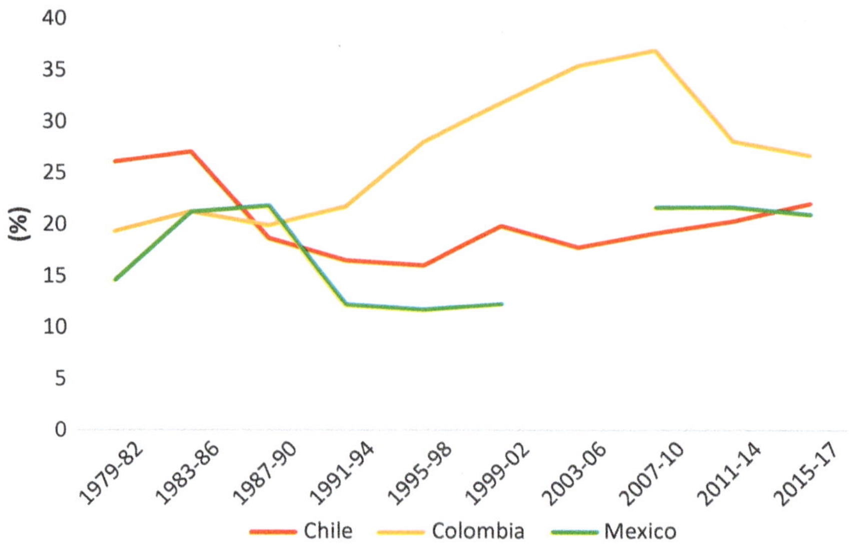

Fig. 7.7 Government expense, 1979–2017 (% of GDP) (Sources: For Colombia between 1975 and 2010: Ocampo (2015, p. 341). For the rest of the years and countries: World Bank (n.d.))
Note: For the case of Mexico, the average between 1999 and 2002 only includes the data for 1999 and 2000. The average between 2007 and 2010 only includes the data for 2008, 2009, and 2010

increased, which contributed to the financial crisis of 1999. This increase was not reversed after the crisis, but instead the government's size continued to grow into the 2000s, which only began to decline again early in the 2010s, although it remained larger than that of Chile and Mexico. To fund the increasing size of the government, including regional and local administrations, operations, and public services, a substantial increase in public resources was required, which explains the multiple tax reforms over the last 40 years.

7.3 Improvements in the Standards of Living in the Twenty-First Century

In the first two decades of the twenty-first century, Colombia witnessed outstanding progress in standards of living for its citizens. The rapid economic growth between 2001 and 2014 allowed the recovery of social

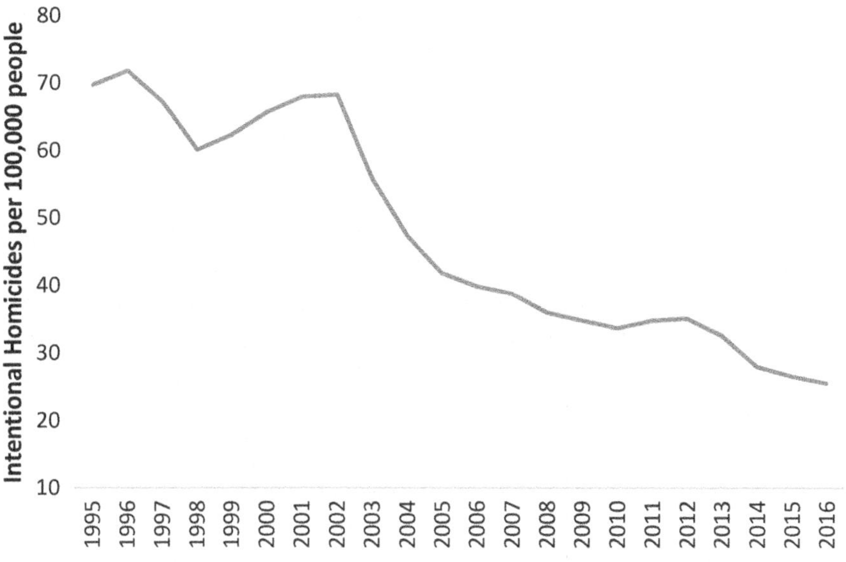

Fig. 7.8 Intentional homicides per 100,000 people, 1995–2016 (Source: World Bank, Global Development Data, n.d.)

indicators that had been affected by the 1999 crisis. In 2001, after two years of serious crisis, the poverty rate measured as a poverty threshold of $5.5 per day (2011 PPP) increased to 60.5%, from 47% in 1992. By the middle of the 2000s, Colombia managed to reduce the poverty rate to the same levels as the early 1990s. The good business cycle continued and a decline in poverty continued, and the figure dipped to 28.7% in 2015.

Likewise, other social indicators saw considerable improvements throughout the early part of the twenty-first century. Life expectancy increased to 74.6 years in 2017, as a result of progress regarding health provision, while schooling saw an outstanding increase, especially in secondary education (as primary schooling surged in the 1950s). The most important achievement in Colombia's recent history was, however, the improvements in security. Figure 7.8 presents the rate of intentional homicide (per 100,000 people) between 1995 and 2016. In the 2000s, Colombia saw a massive reduction in the number of homicides per 100,000 people, reaching a level of 35.9 in 2008, from 68.3 in 2002. This trend extended to the following years, although at a slower pace, until it achieved 25.5 in 2016, a rate still high compared to world standards and far away from being a 'stable' country, but significantly lower than the statistics at the start of the century.

Colombia's rapid economic growth also allowed for an important improvement in income distribution. Inequality is usually seen as a chronic problem in Latin American economies in general, Colombia in particular. Inequality in Colombia is certainly higher than that observed in most other countries, although the Gini coefficient has seen substantial improvement during the twenty-first century. Between 2000 and 2017, Colombia's Gini coefficient reduced by almost 10 points to achieve a level of 49.7 in 2017. This rate is still higher than the values for developed countries, but again, it is significantly better than the figure observed in the early 2000s.

Figure 7.9 presents the Gini index between 1913 and 2017. In analysing these figures, it can be noted that the lowest Gini values (1929, 1980, and 2017) were achieved after periods of rapid economic growth. On the other hand, the Gini worsened during periods of slow economic growth, suggesting a relationship between economic prosperity and inequality. This fact indicates that the probable reason behind the historically high degree of inequality is that the periods of accelerated economic growth did not last long enough to consistently incorporate large enough seg-

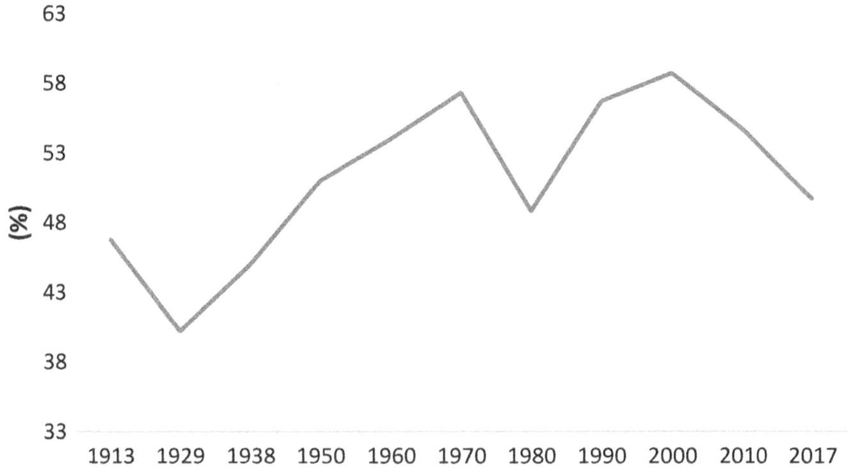

Fig. 7.9 Gini Index, 1913–2017 (%) (Sources: Between 1913 and 1990: Prados de la Escosura (2007); For 2000–2017: World Bank, Global Development Data (n.d.))

ments of the population into the prosperity boom. This was the case for peasants migrating from the countryside to cities in the twentieth century, and the high proportion of the population working in the informal economy in the twenty-first century. In that sense, economic growth seems to be the best policy, not only to generate prosperity, but also to benefit the entire population.

In 2019, Colombia faces a dilemma similar to that of 1930 and 1980. After a period of rapid economic growth, the economy has entered into a slowdown phase which offers the option of either persevering with structural reforms, and embracing the entire potential of the current general purpose technology (ICTs), or delay the implementation of any technological changes which is what ultimately occurred in the past. ICTs offer a window of opportunity for development, as for the innovations in steam and mass production, the sooner any newly available technology is fully taken advantage of, the greater the long-term benefits will be for Colombia.

References

Eslava, M., Garcia, G., Hurtado, B., & Pinzon, A. (2017). *Baja Productividad en Colombia: ¿Un asunto de empresas o de mercado?* Consejo Privado de Competitividad and Universidad de los Andes.

Global Financial Data Finaeon. (n.d.). Global Financial Data Database and Indices. Retrieved from http://www.globalfinancialdata.com/

Maddison Project Database, Version 2018. Bolt, Jutta, Robert Inklaar, Herman de Jong and Jan Luiten van Zanden. (2018). *Rebasing 'Maddison': New Income Comparisons and the Shape of Long-Run Economic Development.* Retrieved from https://www.rug.nl/ggdc/historicaldevelopment/maddison/releases/maddison-project-database-2018

Ocampo, J. (2015). *Historia Económica de Colombia.* Bogota: Fondo de Cultura Económica.

Prados de la Escosura, L. (2007). Inequality and Poverty in Latin America: A Long-Run Exploration. In T. Hatton, K. O'Rourke, & A. Taylor (Eds.), *The New Comparative Economic History. Essays in Honor of Jeffrey G. Williamson.* Cambridge, MA: The MIT Press.

The Conference Board. (n.d.). The Total Economy Database (TED). Byrne and Corrado (2016). *ICT Asset Prices: Marshaling Evidence into New Measures.* EPWP #16-6. Retrieved from https://www.conference-board.org/data/economydatabase/

World Bank, Global Development Data. (n.d.). Retrieved from https://data.worldbank.org/

Epilogue: What Can Be Learned from Colombia?

After analysing Colombia's slow economic growth in the nineteenth century, it can be noted that throughout most of its history, productivity was not the driver for economic growth. Colombia underwent periods of rapid economic expansion, but with the exception of the early twentieth century, input factors were the main drivers behind such progress. What made Colombia's economic growth slow was not the lack of capital and/or labour, but the low efficiency in which it used them. Colombia's slow economic growth was essentially a misallocation problem, in which the country systematically channelled resources towards low-productivity activities.

What lay behind such disappointing productivity performance was the tardy and slow adoption of the three general purpose technologies of the last three centuries: steam, mass production, and ICT. Despite specific circumstances in each historical period, the common pattern of misallocation of resources shaped Colombia's economic history and determined its long-term path of economic growth.

The government played an important role in the slow embrace of the three technological waves. In the late nineteenth century, not paying external debts prevented the country from obtaining the foreign capital that was necessary for the construction of railways. Similarly, protectionism, the external debt default in the 1930s, and excessive government interventionism in credit allocation impeded any rapid absorption of mass

I. Luzardo-Luna, *Colombia's Slow Economic Growth*,
Palgrave Studies in Economic History,
https://doi.org/10.1007/978-3-030-25755-2

production technology during the interwar and import substitution periods.

During the last two decades of the twentieth century, late economic liberalisation and heavy violence prevented any fast formation of ICT capital, reducing its spread in the 2000s. Likewise, the high-tax burden in the twenty-first century maintained many small businesses, especially those in trade, in operating in the informal economy, which slowed down the incorporation of ICT.

At this point, it raises a question regarding what can be learned from Colombia? There are two main conclusions which can be drawn here. The first is that timing matters. The early adoption of the correct policy reduces their payoffs but increases their benefits. In that sense, anticipation is a good course of action, while delaying a corrective measure, or so-called *gradulismo* (gradualism), does not look efficient.

In each one of the episodes presented in this book, Colombia eventually solved what was not working, but the solution came very late, and this reduced their benefits. After avoiding, for what was almost the entire nineteenth century, Colombia finally resumed its external debt repayments in the early twentieth century. The benefits of that policy appeared quickly in the form of railways and an economic take-off. Such benefits were, however, much smaller than those that would have been achieved if the same policy had been implemented in the 1870s. By the 1940s, the railways went into decline, so they were operative for a shorter period than if the network had been built in the late nineteenth century. There is an opportunity cost for delaying a good economic policy.

The second conclusion is optimistic. Against the long-held view in economic history, countries can escape from institutional path dependency. The examples of Argentina in *Belle-Époque*, Mexico in the Second World War, and Chile from the 1980s onwards demonstrate that the way of development is open for these countries able to assume policies that allow for the fast absorption of general purpose technologies. Colombia certainly missed out on the industrial revolution, but it still has time to avoid missing the 5G revolution!

Author Index

I. Luzardo-Luna, *Colombia's Slow Economic Growth*,
Palgrave Studies in Economic History,
https://doi.org/10.1007/978-3-030-25755-2

Subject Index[1]

[1] Note: Page numbers followed by 'n' refer to notes.

I. Luzardo-Luna, *Colombia's Slow Economic Growth*,
Palgrave Studies in Economic History,
https://doi.org/10.1007/978-3-030-25755-2

The manufacturer's authorised representative in the EU is Springer Nature Customer Service Centre GmbH, Europaplatz 3, 69115 Heidelberg, Germany. If you have any concerns regarding our products, please contact ProductSafety@springernature.com

Printed and bound by CPI Group (UK) Ltd, Croydon, CR0 4YY
30/09/2026
02225262-0002